The African American Student's Guide to STEM Careers

D0169045

The African American Student's Guide to STEM Careers

Robert T. Palmer, Andrew T. Arroyo,
and Alonzo M. Flowers III

Foreword by Fred A. Bonner II

 GREENWOOD™

An Imprint of ABC-CLIO, LLC
Santa Barbara, California • Denver, Colorado

Copyright © 2017 by ABC-CLIO, LLC

All rights reserved. No part of this publication may be reproduced, stored in a retrieval system, or transmitted, in any form or by any means, electronic, mechanical, photocopying, recording, or otherwise, except for the inclusion of brief quotations in a review, without prior permission in writing from the publisher.

Library of Congress Cataloging-in-Publication Data

Names: Palmer, Robert T., author. | Arroyo, Andrew T., author. | Flowers, Alonzo M., author.
Title: The African American student's guide to STEM careers / Robert T. Palmer, Andrew T. Arroyo, and Alonzo M. Flowers III ; foreword by Fred A. Bonner II.
Description: Santa Barbara, California : Greenwood, an Imprint of ABC-CLIO, LLC, [2017] | Includes bibliographical references and index.
Identifiers: LCCN 2016032502 (print) | LCCN 2016048249 (ebook) | ISBN 9781610697354 (acid-free paper) | ISBN 9781610697361 (eISBN)
Subjects: LCSH: Science—Vocational guidance—United States. | Technology—Vocational guidance—United States. | Engineering—Vocational guidance—United States. | Mathematics—Vocational guidance—United States. | Minorities—Vocational guidance—United States. | African Americans—Education. | African American students. | African Americans—Employment.
Classification: LCC Q147 .P36 2017 (print) | LCC Q147 (ebook) | DDC 502.3/73—dc23
LC record available at https://lccn.loc.gov/2016032502

ISBN: 978-1-61069-735-4
EISBN: 978-1-61069-736-1

21 20 19 18 17   1 2 3 4 5

This book is also available as an eBook.

Greenwood
An Imprint of ABC-CLIO, LLC

ABC-CLIO, LLC
130 Cremona Drive, P.O. Box 1911
Santa Barbara, California 93116-1911
www.abc-clio.com

This book is printed on acid-free paper (∞)

Manufactured in the United States of America

Contents

Tables and Figures

TABLES

FIGURES

Foreword

The underrepresentation of minorities in STEM is a formidable problem that has plagued the nation for decades, with the past decade presenting some of the most acute issues associated with moving more people of color through the STEM pipeline and ultimately into the STEM workforce. In a recent chapter by Nave et al. (2016), they proffer, regarding their focus on African American student achievement in HBCU STEM programs, "The state of STEM education in the United States is, at best described as improving, and at worst, dismal" (p. 3).

The African American Student's Guide to Stem Careers provides a practical guide that serves as a tool for underrepresented students, particularly Black students who seek critical information to assist them in their efforts to negotiate and navigate the STEM landscape with its variegated terrain. All too often, the information provided to students who seek wise counsel on pursuing careers in STEM disciplines is not grounded nor practical and, thus, not viewed as being accessible or transferable to particular contexts that would assist the student in his or her matriculation in STEM programs.

What makes this book unique is the focus on students and constituents in P–12 and higher education settings. College advisors, counselors, policy makers, teachers, and faculty members—all key individuals who contribute to the matriculation success of Black students in STEM disciplines—are provided with insight to inform them from their particular vantage points. The salience of this text is its "practical utility." This *multicontextual* tome provides key insight through the presentation of not only the authors' *nine key strategies* but also their *15 specific examples* of "real" support systems in both Historically Black College and University (HBCU) and Predominantly White Institution (PWI) settings (Bonner & Murry, 1998; Bonner, Robinson, & Byrd, 2012).

The forward-thinking authors of this book use authentic narrative accounts from STEM professionals who provide their *emic* perspectives on the various challenges and triumphs they have experienced. A classic mantra shared among populations of color who seek to acquire cultural and social capital for the advancement of present and future generations posits, "It is tough to be what you don't see." This book provides a lens through which Black students can bring into clear view their visions of becoming STEM professionals.

I challenge the reader to use this book as a guide that could be read from cover to cover but better serves as a compendium to be studied and used as a resource to tackle issues and unpack stubbornly persistent problems as they relate to the success of Black students in STEM.

Fred A. Bonner II, EdD, Prairie View A&M University

Acknowledgments

Dr. Robert T. Palmer

I want to acknowledge my talented colleagues and friends, Andrew T. Arroyo and Alonzo M. Flowers III, with whom I had the honor and privilege of working on this project.

Dr. Andrew T. Arroyo

I would like to acknowledge the Norfolk State University Department of Interdisciplinary Studies and College of Liberal Arts for the professional flexibility to write a book that crosses disciplinary lines. I would also like to acknowledge Amber Brady, an undergraduate research methods student and aspiring physician assistant (PA), who provided incredible support with formatting references. Finally, I would like to thank Robert T. Palmer for extending the opportunity to coauthor, and Alonzo M. Flowers III for being an outstanding partner on the project.

Dr. Alonzo M. Flowers III

I wish to extend my sincere gratitude to my coauthors Robert T. Palmer and Andrew T. Arroyo for the opportunity to be part of this project and learn from their expertise. I would also like to thank my mentor and friend, Dr. Fred Bonner, for his unwavering support and guidance throughout the years.

How to Use This Book

The African American Student's Guide to STEM Careers is a special book. As expert educators and researchers with decades of experience, we have created this resource with one goal: to increase the number of inspired, prepared Black Americans who earn a STEM degree and enter a STEM profession of their choice. All who share our goal will find value in this book. This includes students, parents, guidance counselors and advisors, teachers and faculty members, researchers, and policy makers.

Although we believe all readers can benefit from reading this book cover to cover, some sections may appeal more to different audiences. Understanding how to use this book should help all types of readers gain the most from it. Anticipating that some sections will appeal to certain readers more than others, we have even taken the special step of altering the style at certain points. We urge readers to consider the following suggestions for how each audience might approach the book for maximum value.

STUDENTS

Our main goal is to guide students, which is reflected in the book's title. As an aid to students, we offer three suggestions. First, refer to the many tables throughout the book. Tables provide convenient summaries of content. The ability to reference the tables quickly will enable students to digest all relevant information from this book so they can put it into practice easily. A list of all tables with page numbers is located on page vii.

Second, read the personal stories from "real-world" STEM professionals. These are found in Chapter Eight. We believe students will gain inspiration and insights by reading these stories. Each contributor identifies as a Black American who has made a contribution in a STEM field.

Third, focus on other key sections and chapters that hold special content for college students. Depending on a student's level—high school, undergraduate, graduate—some parts of the book may be of greatest interest. For example:

- Scholarship information appears on pages 31–38 of Chapter Three. We provide detailed information on 11 scholarships. We also explain graduate assistantships and doctoral fellowships in Chapter Six.

- Predominantly White institutions (PWIs) and historically Black colleges and universities (HBCUs) are discussed on pages 46–51 of Chapter Four. We help students understand some pros and cons of each so they can choose the institution that fits best. Success in the first year of college is enhanced by this choice.

- Also in Chapter Four (beginning on page 51), we offer nine key student-level strategies, practices, and skills that first-year college students need to succeed. Students should return to these over and over again as a refresher to stay on track.

- Institutional support systems to help students through college are discussed beginning on page 64 of Chapter Four. We offer 15 specific examples of real support systems at a variety of colleges and universities. These give students an idea of what is available to them. Even if they do not attend any of the institutions listed, students are informed that these types of systems exist and encouraged to find them wherever they are.

- Choosing a STEM major is covered throughout Chapter Five and then again in Chapter Seven on pages 96–123. We explain the complex nature of what is really involved in declaring a major and progressing through a degree program. We encourage students to return to this material often.

- Graduate school is discussed in Chapter Six. The truth is that many STEM majors should earn an advanced degree because it increases earning potential and opens more doors of real opportunity to become an innovator and leader. We offer practical tips that high school and undergraduate students can use to start targeting a graduate program long before earning their bachelor's degree. Some of these tips are obvious (e.g., grade point average matters), whereas others might not be so obvious (e.g., participate in research conferences). Regardless, students will find all of the tips relevant.

- Careers in STEM are the subject of Chapter Seven. Students will be most interested in the data we provide regarding types of STEM jobs, occupational growth in various sectors, and earning potential. Extensive tables are devoted individually to science, technology, engineering, and mathematics. We also provide a model for framing career success in STEM. Moreover, this chapter inspires and educates students with examples of Black STEM pioneers who accomplished great things in their respective fields.

- Chapter Nine provides a directory of colleges and universities offering STEM programs, along with online resources for exploring STEM. The directory includes the name, the institution type, and Web site for each.

GUIDANCE COUNSELORS AND COLLEGE ADVISORS

Guidance counselors and college advisors can also benefit from this book. If we can deliver one message to counselors and advisors of Black high school and college students, it is this: Black students can succeed in a STEM career. Virtually every successful Black STEM professional has stories of influential counselors and advisors who tried to discourage them from pursuing their dream. We implore every counselor and advisor who reads this book to support and encourage the STEM aspirations of Black students, not to discourage them.

With respect to the current book, counselors and advisors can use it in two ways. First, they can provide it to aspiring Black STEM students as a recommended resource. Using the preceding section as a guide, they can point students to key areas of the book that speak most directly to a pressing need. For example, a struggling student might benefit from the individual success strategies outlined in Chapter Four. Alternatively, a high school student who is interested in learning about careers can examine Chapter Seven. The advisor or counselor can work through the material with the student to form the basis for deeper conversations. Myriad conversation starters are found in these pages.

Second, counselors and advisors can read this book as a form of continuing education or professional development. Whether read privately or utilized as part of a formal departmental, school, or divisional training curriculum, this book contains a wealth of information that every person in a guidance role should know. All well-prepared counselors and advisors should be proficient in every aspect of preparing Black students for STEM majors and careers, and this book can facilitate that proficiency.

TEACHERS AND FACULTY MEMBERS

Teachers and faculty members will find value in this book as well. We suggest using this book in much the same way as counselors and advisors. First, teachers and faculty members can read the book on their own or as part of a training curriculum to become better prepared to assist aspiring Black STEM students. For K–12 teachers, Chapter One is particularly salient. We describe in detail several factors that hinder and promote the success of Black students in STEM at the K–12 level. Specifically, we delineate six factors that hinder participation and six factors that promote success. Then, in Chapter Two, we offer specific information about initiatives in K–12 that contribute to the preparedness of Black STEM students. Because initiatives are adaptable and transferrable across contexts, teachers and faculty members who are eager to set their students up for success can gain valuable ideas from the provided examples. Teachers and faculty members might be surprised to learn of the various challenges facing their Black students, prompting changes to their own practice in response.

Second, teachers and faculty members can give this book to students as a resource for their development. If used in this fashion, we suggest pointing students to the areas that are of most interest to them. Because a student or faculty member knows their students, they will be able to judge which sections of the book are most applicable. Alternatively, they can use our suggestions in the earlier section on how students can read this book. This process can benefit both parties as they engage in honest conversations about challenges and solutions for Black STEM student success.

RESEARCHERS AND POLICY MAKERS

Researchers and policy makers can benefit from this book too. Policy makers, in particular, will be interested in Chapters One and Two. As persons with the authority and responsibility for shaping the institutional pipelines that can facilitate or frustrate the entry of Black STEM students into degree programs and careers, the ideas contained in these chapters can inform a host of decisions. Staffing; resource allocation for recruitment, retention, or support programs; and strategic direction for institutions can all be strengthened by attention to the issues raised in this book.

Finally, researchers can strengthen their work by reading this book. Although our primary audience is students and practitioners, we see potential value for researchers on two fronts. First, the book might spark ideas for further investigation. We have grounded the content in the research literature and arranged the material in such a way that researchers might find concepts and connections they did not consider before. Second, and just as important, we encourage education researchers to publish reader-friendly work that appeals to the public. If scholarship is limited to the narrow readership of experts, then it falls short of effecting change. In addition, if the topic of the scholarship is about the need for change—for example, an increase in Black STEM students and professionals—then researchers can help generate change by writing for broader audiences.

In conclusion, we hope this book will make a positive contribution to a variety of readers. It is different from many other books, which should allow it to fill a niche. We hope readers will agree.

Robert T. Palmer, PhD
Andrew T. Arroyo, EdD
Alonzo M. Flowers III, PhD

INTRODUCTION

The Importance of STEM to Black Students

Within the past few years, a significant number of articles, policy reports, book chapters, and other publications have highlighted the importance of science, technology, engineering, and, mathematics (STEM) to the economy of the United States (Dancy, 2010; Guess, 2008; Moore, 2006; Öztürk, 2007; Palmer, Davis, & Thompson, 2010). These sources commonly note that America's competitiveness in the global economy is tied to its production of workers with training in scientific and technological areas. Despite this, many countries are outpacing the United States in regards to workers with skills in scientific and technological capacities. Currently, 13 countries outrank the United States in the ratio of students who receive their first degree in natural science and engineering (Palmer, Maramba, & Dancy, 2011). Meanwhile, degree attainment in science and engineering fields among students in the United States has dropped in many areas of the physical sciences, engineering, mathematics, and computer science at the undergraduate and graduate level (Museus, Palmer, Davis, & Maramba, 2011). One of the factors contributing to America's low production of workers with training in the STEM fields is the nation's changing demography (U.S. Census Bureau, 2012). According to numerous sources (e.g., Chang, Cerna, Han, & Sàenz, 2008; Cole & Espinoza, 2008; Leslie, McClure, & Oaxaca, 1998; Museus et al., 2011), Black, Hispanic, Asian, and Native American populations are expected to grow rapidly over the next few decades while the White population is expected to decline. In fact, those populations will comprise approximately 50 percent of the total U.S. population by 2050, a trend already playing out in several states (Palmer, Maramba, & Holmes, 2011). Given the changing demography of the United States, coupled with the fact that the "new majority" (Rendón & Hope, 1996) has been historically underrepresented in STEM, more attention must be devoted to increasing the preparedness and success of this new emerging demographic majority in STEM

(Dancy, 2010; Guess, 2008; Moore, 2006; Öztürk, 2007; Palmer, Davis, Moore, & Hilton, 2010).

Although the changing U.S. demographics and the need to ensure America's competitiveness in the global marketplace are two critical reasons more efforts must be aimed at increasing the preparedness of underrepresented minorities in STEM, a more fundamental reason lies in the fact that the population comprising the new majority continues to suffer from persisting systemic inequities in the K–12 educational system. To this end, increasing the preparedness and success of the new majority in STEM is both a moral and ethical imperative (Museus et al., 2011). In addition to the aforementioned factors, the preparedness of underrepresented minorities in STEM has implications for their financial well-being. For example, the annual income of high school graduates on average is about 62 percent to that of college graduates (Museus et al., 2011). Consequently, the success of minorities in STEM will manifest into greater individual and economic rewards.

While we acknowledge that racial and ethnic minorities are underrepresented in STEM, this book is focused on Black students. Nevertheless, many of the issues discussed throughout this book bear relevance to other underrepresented racial minorities. However, the focus on Black students is quite timely as an article from *U.S. News and World Report* points out that Black students in general and Black men specifically are perhaps one of the most underrepresented demographics in STEM (Bidwell, 2015). An article from *Huffington Post* echoes this sentiment and indicates that the percentage of Blacks who earn degrees in STEM has declined during the past decades (Washington, 2011). Specifically, this article stated:

> From community college through PhD level, the percentage of STEM degrees received by Blacks in 2009 was 7.5 percent, down from 8.1 percent in 2001. The numbers are striking in certain fields. In 2009, African-Americans received 1 percent of degrees in science technologies, and 4 percent of degrees in math and statistics. Out of 5,048 PhDs awarded in the physical sciences, such as chemistry and physics, 89 went to African-Americans—less than 2 percent.

Given the dearth of participation among Black students in STEM, we compose this book with the goal of helping to increase the engagement of Black students in STEM education. Specifically, this book's nine chapters each provide critical information to help increase the participation and success of this demographic group in STEM. While we will provide more information about the coming chapters in the subsequent sections of this book, we first want to define what STEM is. Doing so is important because while many academic and nonacademic publications underscore the importance of STEM, few resources give context to what STEM actually is.

WHAT IS STEM?

The National Science Foundation (2010a), as well as other academic publications (e.g., Museus et al., 2011), notes that STEM is comprised of the following:

1. **Science fields**: These fields include environmental (earth sciences, oceanography), life (agricultural, biological, medical sciences), and physical (astronomy, chemistry, physics) sciences.
2. **Technology fields**: These fields include computer sciences (computer and information science as well as management information systems).
3. **Engineering fields**: These fields include aeronautical, astronautical, bioengineering and biomedical, chemical, civil, electrical, and mechanical engineering.
4. **Mathematics fields**: These fields include general mathematics, applied mathematics, and mathematical statistics.

Although not explicitly recognized by the National Science Foundation as a discipline in STEM, the American Psychological Association (APA) has classified psychology as a STEM discipline. According to Bray (2010), there is some contention in the STEM profession about the recognition of psychology as a STEM discipline. However, in a report entitled *Psychology as a Core Science, Technology, Engineering, and Mathematics (STEM) Discipline*, Bray argues that psychology should be included as a STEM discipline because it contributes directly to scientific and technological innovations as well as indirectly to "education and learning in science and technology" (p. 2).

Specifically, Bray posits that psychological science not only helps to facilitate designing new technologies but also promotes public safety with innovations, improves public health with applied research, and leads to the development of educational techniques that contribute to students' mastery of mathematic and scientific learning. Given this argument, in this book, we have included psychology as a discipline in STEM. However, we also recognize the tension surrounding this dilemma.

This introduction has discussed the importance of STEM to the nation's economic interest as well as its significance to the new majority in general and Blacks specifically. It has also provided context regarding what fields and discipline are inclusive of STEM. In the first chapter of this book, *Planning for a Career in STEM*, we will discuss factors at the K–12 level to help prepare Black students for college majors in STEM. This chapter will stress that sufficient academic preparation, particularly in math and science, at the K–12 level is critical for success in STEM majors at the collegiate level. This chapter will also highlight critical factors that support or hinder the success of Black STEM students. Embedded in each chapter will be a table that outlines the major issues addressed.

CHAPTER ONE

Planning for a Career in STEM

The purpose of this chapter is to discuss factors in K–12 that support or hinder the academic success of Black students who desire to major in STEM in higher education. Discussing these factors is critical because they provide important context that will help Black students plan for a career in STEM. In addition to discussing these factors, we also provide recommendations to educators regarding how they might use these factors to help promote the interest and success of Black students in STEM. Therefore, this chapter may be of most interest to educators who are in a position to influence the direction of Black students at the K–12 level.

ACADEMIC PREPAREDNESS

Research illustrates that success in STEM is based on adequate academic preparation for college-level work in STEM. Despite the salient connection between academic preparation in K–12 and success in STEM, Black students are limited in mathematics and science courses in K–12. Bonous-Hammarth (2000), who examined a nationally representative sample using cross tabulations, factor analyses, and logistic regressions, found that Black undergraduates were less likely to be retained in science, mathematics, and engineering majors in college compared to their White and Asian American counterparts because they were inadequately prepared in K–12 to succeed in these subjects. In the next section, we turn to a discussion of factors that hinder Black students' academic preparedness for college-level work in STEM.

FACTORS IN K–12 THAT HINDER THE PREPARATION OF BLACK STUDENTS IN STEM

Research indicates that insufficient academic preparation among Black students in science and mathematics in K–12 education is coupled tightly to their lack of success in STEM education. Accordingly, in this section, we highlight six factors in K–12 that contribute to the inadequate academic preparation of Black students in STEM. Specifically, we discuss the following (1) school district funding disparities, (2) tracking into remedial courses, (3) underrepresentation in advanced placement courses, (4) unqualified teachers in K–12, (5) low teacher expectations, and (6) oppositional culture.

School District Funding Disparities

One factor that contributes to the underpreparedness of Black students in STEM is disparities in school funding. In many cases, schools are funded through local property taxes, which means schools in more affluent neighborhoods receive more funding per pupil than schools in less wealthy communities. This puts Blacks and other low-income students at a disadvantage because they are more likely to live in inner cities and underresourced communities. For example, data show that, while 3 percent of White eighth graders are in schools where more than 75 percent of the students qualify for free or reduced lunch, 35 percent of eighth-grade Blacks and 34 percent of Hispanics are in such schools (Flores, 2007). Due to this funding system and the fact that many Black students are more likely to come from less affluent communities, school districts that serve a large number of Blacks and Hispanics receive less local and state funding to educate students, compared with school districts that serve a low percentage of racial and ethnic minority students.

The funding disparity between school districts goes hand in hand with the kind of resources their schools are able to provide for students. For example, schools with more resources often offer smaller classes, which positively contribute to student learning and achievement. This puts Black students at a disadvantage, given that they disproportionately attend schools with fewer resources and, therefore, larger class sizes. Moreover, because Black students attend K–12 schools that receive less funding, these schools typically are not able to provide the latest books, laboratories, instructional material, and technology as those schools that receive more funding.

Tracking into Remedial Courses

Another systemic factor that contributes to the disproportionate underpreparedness of Black students in STEM is academic tracking. *Academic tracking* is the schools' systematic placement of students in classes based on their performance on standardized testing or teachers' perceptions of their academic ability. Such tracking promotes the inequality of Black students because students who are placed in high-achieving academic tracks are exposed to more complex and challenging classroom instruction than those who are placed in low-achieving academic tracks. For example, Gamoran, Porter, Smithson, and White (1997) conducted a study using data from school districts in San Francisco and San Diego, California, and Rochester and Buffalo, New York, to examine academic tracking. The researchers selected these districts because they were urban districts with a high percentage of low-achieving students and had recently implemented new mathematics initiatives. They found that students in high-achieving academic tracks learned more than students in low-achieving academic tracks. To this end, the authors concluded, "General-track math classes should be eliminated. Instruction is weak, achievement is shallow, and general math is a dead end for students' mathematics careers" (p. 333).

Moreover, existing empirical research shows that Black students are overrepresented in low-ability or remedial tracks, even when their scores on standardized assessments are equal to or better than their White peers. In a comprehensive review of the literature on women and racial and ethnic minority students in science and mathematics, Oakes (1990) noted that Blacks and Hispanics are tracked into remedial courses in elementary schools, which subsequently makes it difficult for them to succeed in mathematics and science courses as they advance through the education system. Because tracking hinders Black students' ability to learn advanced science and mathematics, it is an important barrier to educational equity.

Underrepresentation in Advanced Placement Courses

Whereas Black students are overrepresented in remedial courses, they are underrepresented in advanced placement (AP) courses. Adelman (2006) provided evidence of the disparity in access to AP courses suffered by racial and ethnic minority students using nationally representative data. Specifically, he found that compared to White students, Blacks are far less likely to attend high schools that offer AP courses in subjects such as trigonometry and calculus. Similarly, Ladson-Billings (1997) explains that schools which disproportionately serve a large number of Black students tend to have "less demanding mathematics programs and offer fewer opportunities for students to take such gatekeeper courses as algebra and calculus that lead to increased opportunities at the college level and beyond" (p. 701). This underrepresentation in AP courses is important because college preparatory coursework has a positive impact on a variety of achievement outcomes, such as higher scores on standardized college entrance assessments and more completed years of education. Thus, the underrepresentation of Blacks in AP courses negatively influences their preparation and subsequent success.

Even when AP courses in mathematics and science are available, many Black students do not engage in them for several reasons. First, Black students do not view these courses as relevant to their future educational and career trajectories. Second, many Black students view courses in advanced mathematics and science as difficult and do not believe it is worth investing additional time to do well in them. Even though Blacks plan to pursue scientific careers in numbers similar to Whites, because they are not adequately prepared academically, they abandon their pursuit of science careers after they start to encounter more challenging courses. Third, math anxiety can cause Black students to avoid participating in advanced mathematics and science courses. Finally, perhaps the most critical cause of the underrepresentation of Black students in AP courses is their elementary and junior high school experiences. That is, because a disproportionate percentage of Blacks have been placed in remedial or general mathematics and science tracks, as we discussed in the previous section, they are ill prepared to succeed in more rigorous mathematics and science courses in high school and beyond.

Educators can do a number of things to help promote the engagement of Black students in AP courses. For example, they could help demystify the fear associated with AP courses that some students, particularly Black students, may have about these courses by simply talking to students and telling them about the benefits of AP courses. They could also emphasize how these courses will help students' preparedness for college and beyond, particularly if they major and work in a STEM profession. They could also allow students who are interested in AP courses, but are afraid of enrolling in such courses, to sit in on an AP course to see if they like it. Moreover, if an educator notices students excelling in mathematics or science courses, the educator should encourage those students to take the AP course. Finally, because the systemic tracking of Black students into remedial or low-ability courses serves as the culprit for their underpreparedness for AP courses, educators should determine if they have policies in their school that are disadvantageous to a group of students. If so, perhaps they should form a committee that works to dismantle these policies and place students in the appropriate educational setting to help increase the achievement and success of Black students in general, specifically those interested in mathematics and science.

Unqualified Teachers in K–12

The underrepresentation of qualified teachers among educators who serve large numbers of Black students is another contributor to their lack of academic preparedness in STEM. A report from the National Science Board (2010) underscores the severity of Black students not having equal access to qualified teachers in mathematics and science. For example, the report noted that, in 2004, White fifth graders were 51 percent more likely to be taught by teachers with a master's or advanced degree than their Black and Hispanic peers. Similarly, Flores (2007) explained that students attending predominantly Black schools are twice as likely to be taught by teachers with three years of teaching experience or less, compared to those attending predominantly White schools.

Evidence regarding the impact of teacher preparation on student outcomes is generally consistent in its indication that teacher qualifications in the subject they teach does, in fact, affect success among all students in STEM education. Research on this topic suggests that students who are taught by individuals with a degree in the subject are more likely to have more positive educational outcomes. For example, using data from the National Education Longitudinal Study of 1988 (NELS:88), Goldhaber and Brewer (2000) found that math students who were instructed by teachers with baccalaureate or master's degrees in mathematics had higher test scores compared to students who were taught by teachers with out-of-subject degrees.

Low Teacher Expectations

In addition to unqualified teachers, researchers have also discussed that teachers' low expectations can hinder the achievement of Black students in math and science courses. Moreover, the relationship between teacher expectations and academic achievement appears to be a reciprocal one. That is, while teacher expectations influence academic achievement, students' academic performance can also affect teachers' expectations of those pupils. Indeed, teachers maybe more likely to develop expectations about students and treat them in a manner that is more consistent with their performance on a standardized assessment than their actual abilities. Thus, given that Black students are likely to perform lower on standardized math and science examinations than their majority counterparts, teachers are more likely to have higher expectations for White students than for minority students.

In turn, research demonstrates that teacher expectations can influence academic performance, suggesting that those expectations can become a self-fulfilling prophecy for students. More specifically, mathematics and science courses are viewed as higher-order disciplines, and teachers are inclined to perceive Black students as lacking ability in those areas and send subtle messages that such disciplines are White male domains. Such messages can lead to differences in teaching behavior and subsequent achievement. In addition, Black students, in particular, seem to be influenced by what they believe teachers think of them and their ability to succeed in mathematics and science courses. Although existing research shows that teachers' expectations can have a negative impact on the academic success of Black students in STEM, it also indicates that caring teachers can have a positive impact on the academic preparedness and success of racial and ethnic minority students in those fields. Given the important role that expectations of educators have on student achievement, educators should attempt to have high expectations for all students with whom they come in contact. If their biases or cultural prejudices prevent this from happening, perhaps they should seek counseling or have a neutral and objective party, preferably someone of a minority background, visit their classroom to observe the manner in which they interact with students. Doing so will help the educator see implicit biases that he or she may not be aware of and ensure that all students are held to the same expectations in an equal and fair manner.

Oppositional Culture

Researchers have also implicated oppositional culture for the negative academic outcomes of Blacks in K–12. Oppositional culture is a theory that Fordham and

Ogbu (1986) proposed to explain the academic disengagement of Black students. The authors explain that Blacks have formed a culture in opposition to mainstream values and norms, stemming from the racial oppression, enslavement, and discrimination they have experienced. This oppositional culture acts as a barrier between Blacks and Whites, and it provokes Blacks to persuade their same-race peers to devalue academic success because of its association with "acting White."

Several researchers have expressed concern about oppositional culture as an explanation of the academic disparities faced by Blacks. Notwithstanding the criticism, some support does exist for the theory's relevancy in accounting for the disparity in educational outcomes for Black students. Although there is criticism about oppositional culture, this theory could be used to explain the negative educational outcomes of Blacks in K–12, particularly in STEM education. This literature on oppositional culture highlights the importance of educators and school personnel in K–12 encouraging all students, especially Black students, to be cognizant of the relationship between peer interaction and academic achievement. As mentioned previously, although there is criticism about the impact the oppositional culture has on the success of Black students, some research supports the linkage between peer influence and "acting White." Given this, educators should openly discuss with students how peer association could enhance or limit student success in general and Black students specifically. Aside from having discussions, they could also use the hidden curriculum (e.g., posting signs around the classroom) to try to teach students about the relationship between peer associations and academic success.

This chapter has discussed factors that hinder the academic success of Black students who desire to major in STEM at the college level. Table 1.1 provides a brief summary of those factors.

In summary, research indicates that academic preparedness in K–12 is crucial for Black students to be successful in STEM. However, many of those students are insufficiently prepared to succeed in STEM. To enhance the participation and success of Black students in STEM education, it is critical to mitigate the factors that negatively impact the success of Black students in K–12. In the remaining section of this chapter, we focus on factors in K–12 that contribute to the success of Black students in STEM.

Table 1.1   Factors in K–12 That Hinder the Participation of Black Students in STEM

Lack of a strong academic foundation in mathematics and science courses
Attending underfunded/underresourced schools
Lacking access to teachers certified to teach mathematics and science courses
Lack of participation in AP courses
Being tracked into low ability courses
Low teacher expectations for the academic success of Black students
Oppositional culture (e.g., "acting" White)

FACTORS IN K–12 THAT PROMOTE THE SUCCESS OF BLACK STUDENTS IN STEM

Along with the variables in K–12 that hinder the academic preparation of Black students in STEM, educational researchers have also identified six factors in K–12 that contribute to success among minority students. In this section, we discuss those six factors: (1) parental expectations and involvement, (2) authentic science engagement and active learning, (3) culturally relevant teaching, (4) early exposure to careers in STEM, (5) interest in STEM, and (6) self-efficacy in STEM.

Parental Expectations and Involvement

A number of researchers have expressed that parental expectations and involvement can facilitate the success of Black students in STEM. Russell and Atwater (2005), for example, interviewed 11 Black college students attending a predominantly White institution (PWI) to gain insight into factors that led them to pursue and persist in STEM majors. They highlighted the importance of the participants' parents emphasizing the significance of a good education and having high expectations while the students were in either primary or secondary schools. Participants also credited their parents for helping them develop good study skills. Similarly, a study that Moore (2006) conducted with 42 Black males in engineering revealed how the participants' parents impacted their desire to pursue engineering in college.

Authentic Science Engagement and Active Learning

Aside from high parental expectations and involvement, research has shown that authentic engagement in science helps to facilitate the interest and success of Black students in STEM. *Authentic science engagement* is defined as discovery-based research courses as opposed to standard laboratory courses. This type of instructional approach encourages students to be deeply engaged in the learning experience because it promotes individual ownership of projects "and provides a direct way for students to experience real discovery and innovation" (Institute for Broadening Participation, 2014b). According to scholarship, when Blacks and other minorities perceive their science, mathematics, or engineering coursework as enjoyable, those students are much more inclined to persist in their chosen field. Connected to this pedagogical approach of authentic engagement in science is active learning. *Active learning* replaces laboratory instruction and lecturing with hands-on learning. Studies have shown that active learning improves retention of information and facilitates critical thinking skills, all of which play an important role in the success of STEM majors in college.

With these two approaches in mind, educators can design their classrooms to foster student interest and resiliency in STEM education through student-driven, project-based learning. Teachers can also provide regular opportunities for authentic student-led inquiry, which will help expand or enrich students' interest in technical explorations and distinctions that engender resiliency, creativity, and curiosity. These characteristics are vital because they are necessary for success in STEM majors and careers, particular as students begin to define and refine their identity as self-perceptions in STEM.

Culturally Relevant Teaching

In addition to authentic science engagement and active learning, scholars have discussed the role of culturally relevant pedagogy in facilitating the success of Black students in mathematics and science in K–12 education. Ladson-Billings (1995b) asserted that culturally relevant pedagogical practices must meet three criteria: they must focus on (1) developing students academically, (2) nurturing and supporting students' cultural competence, and (3) developing students' critical competence. Lipman (1995) conducted an ethnographic study of three Black teachers and provided a concrete example of culturally relevant pedagogy for Black students. Specifically, Lipman indicated that the teachers held high expectations for all students and instilled in them that they all had the desire and potential to learn. They also established meaningful commitments and relationships with students' families to help facilitate the students' academic achievement. In addition, the teachers validated the students' non-Eurocentric lives. Finally, they celebrated the richness of the students' language, culture, and experience.

Culturally relevant pedagogy is an important consideration because when science and math teachers instruct from a Eurocentric point of view, they fail to include an approach that connects curriculum, instruction, and assessment to the experiences, cultures, and traditions of Black students. Such Eurocentric pedagogy imposes racial inferiority on minority students and causes those students to view mathematics as a subject that is exclusively for White males, hindering those students' ability to see the applicability of science and mathematics to their own lives. Thus, it is important to consider the role of culturally relevant pedagogy in efforts to serve Black students.

Research illustrates that incorporating culturally relevant pedagogy into science and mathematics instruction has a positive impact on Black students. Denson, Avery, and Schell (2010), for example, conducted a study of seven Black high school students regarding their perception of engineering and found that using culturally relevant pedagogy in K–12 was important to attracting those students to engineering programs. In addition, Tate (1995a) provided further evidence of the utility of incorporating culturally relevant pedagogy into mathematics instruction by explaining how one teacher had a positive impact on students' interest and success in mathematics by including social issues that Blacks often encounter in education and society into her pedagogical practices.

Educators can demonstrate culturally relevant pedagogy in the classroom in the following ways:

• Learning more about students and building on their interest and linguistic resources

- Learning more about students' community and home resources, providing an opportunity that enables students to examine the curriculum from multiple various ous
- Using different assessment tools that promote student learning; using examples and analogies that are indicative of the students' culture
- Developing positive and supportive relationships with students' guardians and community figures
- Helping students find meaning in what they learned
- Preparing students to be change agents in their communities

Early Exposure to Careers in STEM

Research also indicates that there is a relationship between early exposure to science and mathematics careers and long-term success in STEM (Museus, Palmer, Davis, & Maramba, 2011). It has been suggested that when Black students have greater access to information about careers in STEM and quality career guidance, they are more inclined to develop interests in mathematics and science fields. Thus, such access and guidance might be critical in fostering Black students' interest in STEM.

One way to expose Black students to STEM careers early on is through connecting with role models in those professions. Access and exposure to role models is important because visualizing or seeing people who achieve positive outcomes (e.g., attaining a professional position in the STEM workforce) can raise students' self-efficacy, or beliefs that they too can achieve those outcomes. Several people in the STEM fields have asserted that the availability of role models could be one factor that facilitates the success of Black students in STEM (Muesus, Palmer, Davis, & Maramba, 2011).

However, although researchers have provided evidence of the significant impact that teachers and counselors can have on Black students' success in STEM, evidence that highlights the impact of minority role models—that is, individuals who model minority success in STEM professions—is difficult to find. Research does suggest that having parents who are STEM professionals is correlated with success in STEM education, but the actual effects of nonparent role models are uncertain (Muesus, Palmer, Davis, & Maramba, 2011).

Interest in STEM

In addition to the connection between early exposure to STEM fields and success in STEM, research shows that there is a relationship between Black students having an interest in mathematics and science in K–12 and their persistence and success in STEM. For example, Hall and Post-Kammer (1987) reported that early interest in science is positively related to students' desires to major in science in college. Similarly, Hrabowski and Maton (1995) explained that interest in science is one predictor of future academic success in the physical sciences. Furthermore, in Moore's (2006) study of 42 Black engineering students who were attending a PWI, participants expressed that having a passion for engineering and mathematics in primary and secondary school contributed to their persistence in higher education.

Although interest in STEM majors or careers is an important precursor to the success of Black students in STEM, it should be noted that a lack of interest in those careers does not appear to be the primary source of the high departure rates of Black students from STEM education. One thing educators can do to help increase interest in STEM is reading biographies of Black scientists to the Black students. According to research from the Institute for Broadening Participation (2014b), "simply reading to students biographies of scientists from underrepresented groups increased [their] science aspiration" (p. 6). To learn about the breadth and depth of biographies of Black scientists, educators can visit The History Makers: Science Makers Web site (http://www.thehistorymakers.com/makers/science makers). This Web site provides context on more than 180 Black notable scientists. Not only do these narratives serve as resources for students, but they also provide them with role models and possibly pique their interest in a career in STEM. Moreover, in Chapter Seven of this book, we provide examples of prominent Black individuals who greatly impacted different professional areas in STEM.

Self-Efficacy in STEM

Another conclusion drawn from existing research is that Black students' self-efficacy in STEM, or confidence in their ability to do math and science in primary and secondary education, is a salient predictor of success in STEM education. For instance, using data from the 1971 and 1980 Cooperative Institutional Research Program (CIRP), Leslie, McClure, and Oaxaca (1998) found that self-efficacy is an important predictor of success in STEM for racial and ethnic minority students. In addition, using the NELS (88:00) data, Holt (2006) noted a relationship between racial and ethnic minority high school students' confidence in their ability to do well in mathematics and enrollment in higher-level mathematics courses. Holt further explained that students' confidence in their ability to do well in mathematics was a predictor of persistence in STEM education.

The impact of Black students' self-efficacy—or confidence in their ability—on their success in STEM is complicated when considering it simultaneously with other factors. According to Seymour and Hewitt (1997), Blacks experience a conflict between overconfidence and poor preparation, which impairs their success in STEM. More specifically, they explained that many minority students who major in STEM in college come from high schools where they were viewed as academically superior compared to their peers. In these schools, they developed strong confidence but lacked advanced skills that are necessary to achieve their aspirations because of their lack of participation in AP classes. As a result, when those students entered college, they were overwhelmed and at greater risk of switching to less intense majors or dropping out of college.

To enhance the self-efficacy of Black students in STEM, educators can design interventions to psychologically combat negative stereotypes that can engender low-efficacy or stereotype threat. *Stereotype threat* is a phenomenon that causes Black students as well as other minorities (e.g., women) to question their ability to perform well in academic tasks because of the prevalence of stereotypes about their efforts to be academically successful. Research has shown that such interventions can be successful in lessening stereotype threat. For example, Good, Aronson, and Inzlicht (2003) randomly assigned 138 seventh-grade students to four groups being mentored by college students to understand if mentoring would improve gender stereotypes and lessen the gender gap in mathematical test scores in the sample. While the first group learned about the expandable nature of intelligence, the second group learned that everyone encountered challenges when they transitioned into seventh grade, but things would get better. In the third group, students learned a mixture of the first two messages. These three groups were compared with the fourth group at the conclusion of the school year, and the researchers discerned that, in all three groups, the gender gap disappeared.

SUMMARY OF THE FACTORS IN K–12 THAT FACILITATE THE SUCCESS OF BLACK STUDENTS IN STEM

In the preceding section, we critically reviewed and provided context on the factors that enabled the participation as well as the success of Blacks in STEM at the K–12 level. In Table 1.2, we summarize those factors.

CONCLUDING THOUGHTS

In summary, research shows that many factors in K–12 are instrumental in helping facilitate the success of Black students in STEM. Being aware of these factors could play a critical role in helping educators enhance the success of Black students in STEM. In the next chapter, *Preparing for Success in STEM: Initiatives at the K–12 Level That Contribute to the Preparedness of Black STEM Students*, we delineate initiatives in K–12 to enhance the preparedness and success of Black students in STEM. Focusing on these initiatives is important because they provide

Table 1.2   Factors in K–12 That Facilitate the Success of Black Students in STEM

Parental expectations and involvement
Authentic engagement in science and active learning
Culturally relevant teaching (e.g., teaching that incorporates aspects of the child's culture into the curriculum)
Early Exposure to careers in STEM
Interest in STEM
Self-efficacy (e.g., confidence) in STEM

educators and students alike with programs that help increase the preparedness of Black students who will major in STEM in postsecondary education.

NOTE

Portions of this chapter have been adapted from Museus, S. D., Palmer, R. T., Davis, R. J., & Maramba, D. C. (2011). *Racial and ethnic minority students' success in STEM education.* Hoboken, NJ: Jossey-Bass. Used by permission.

CHAPTER TWO

Preparing for Success in STEM: Initiatives at the K–12 Level That Contribute to the Preparedness of Black STEM Students

This chapter highlights and discusses initiatives at the K–12 level that facilitate the preparedness and success of Black students in STEM. According to a review of literature, a litany of programs at the K–12 level help engender the success of students in STEM. Reviewing these programs is beneficial because research has shown that high-quality STEM programs can improve students' attitudes toward STEM fields and careers, increase STEM knowledge and skills, and enhance students' likelihood of graduating and pursuing a career in STEM. Thus, by reviewing these programs, we hope to provide practitioners with concrete examples of how some educators have created supportive structures that may increase success for Black students in STEM. Specifically, we focus on seven programs: the (1) Pre-Engineering Program at the University of Akron, (2) Detroit Area Pre-College Engineering Program (DAPCEP), (3) Say YES to a Youngster's Future, (4) the STEM Institute, (5) the Tech Apprentice Program, (6) Metro Early College High School, and (7) the AP STEM Access Program. If these programs provided empirical evidence to gauge their efficacy as well as the methodology used in the programs' assessment, we included this information because it gives educators, students, and researchers keener insight into these programmatic initiatives.

PRE-ENGINEERING PROGRAM AT THE UNIVERSITY OF AKRON

The University of Akron has promulgated an initiative to increase the enrollment and success of first-generation college students (e.g., neither parent having earned a bachelor's degree) of Black students in STEM. More specifically, the University has established a Pre-Engineering Program, which functions as a summer-and after-school program. The goals of this program include reinforcing the self-confidence of Black high school students in STEM, enhancing their problem-solving abilities, increasing their awareness of careers in STEM, using diagnostic testing to identify deficiencies, and providing students with opportunities to use computers and become familiar with the use of word processing, spreadsheets, mathematics software, and the Internet.

Approximately 40 students in grades 9 through 12 are admitted into the Pre-Engineering Program each year. Participants must meet the following criteria: live in Ohio, Pennsylvania, Indiana, or Michigan; demonstrate interest or potential in advanced placement courses in mathematics or science; demonstrate a level of maturity and independence to enable them to live away from home for six weeks; and meet federal poverty guidelines. In addition, prospective students must achieve a GPA of 2.5, attend a conference with parents, and engage in an interview with the director of the program. Students or their families are not financially responsible for participating in the program. The U.S. Department of Education covers all necessary student expenses. Students who are formally admitted to the program receive a weekly stipend during the summer and a monthly stipend during the year.

For six weeks during the summer, selected students participate in a series of academic classes, such as English, mathematics, physics, biology, and a foreign language. Simultaneously, the program participants interact with engineering faculty and staff for about an hour and a half daily. In this summer program, participants work collaboratively with faculty and staff on building projects, laboratory demonstrations, and other structured learning activities. Faculty members also provide students with advice on career planning and mentoring. In addition to collaborative experiences with faculty, students work collectively with each other on projects such as designing bridges, building model roller coasters, designing rockets, testing building materials, and designing electronic circuits.

Aside from the summer program, students also participate in a series of career workshops at regional manufacturing companies and research facilities and attend weekly tutoring sessions throughout the school year. These workshops expose students to STEM careers. Furthermore, they provide an opportunity for students to have one-on-one discussions with the engineers. For participants who are out of state, the Internet serves as a conduit through which they can participate. The tutoring occurs in partnership with the College of Engineering at the University of Akron. More specifically, engineering students from the Increasing Diversity in Engineering Academics (IDEA) program and student members of the National Society of Black Engineers (NSBE) volunteer six hours per week to provide mentorship for participants of the pre-engineering programs.

Lam, Strivatsan, Doverspike, Vesalo, and Ruby-Mawasha (2005) argued that the Pre-Engineering Program has been tremendously successful. More specifically, they found that 100 percent of the program's participants graduated from high school, and 94 percent of those students entered college. Furthermore, the authors concluded the following:

> The University of Akron summer integrated and year-round academic programs have increased access and retention of identifiable under-represented

students pursuing STEM careers. . . . The pre-engineering curricula actually results in several significant students outcomes such as (1) increase[d] grade point average, (2) less anxiety toward math and science, (3) fostering the can-do attitude, and (4) increasing personal self-esteem. (p. 18)

DETROIT AREA PRE-COLLEGE ENGINEERING PROGRAM

Another program in K–12 that focuses on increasing the enrollment and success of Black students in the STEM is the Detroit Area Pre-College Engineering Program (DAPCEP) (Hill, 1990). Implemented with a grant from the Alfred P. Sloan Foundation in 1976, the DAPCEP works in concert with the Detroit Public School System, local universities, major corporations, and businesses to increase the number of middle and high school students interested in pursuing STEM careers for Detroit.

The DAPCEP provides instructional and motivational activities throughout the school year and during the summer for Black students in grades 7–12. More specifically, the DAPCEP includes three interrelated components: the Summer Skill Intensification program, which offers classes in mathematics, science, computer science, and communication in grades 9–12; Saturday enrichment classes, which are held at several area universities and consist of courses in physics, chemistry, laboratory science, technical writing, engineering (chemical, civil, electrical, and mechanical), algebra, trigonometry, calculus, and computer science; and pre-engineering classes in science and engineering that are held at public schools in Detroit. In such classes, students participate in science fairs, attend field trips, view presentations by technical speakers, research minority engineers and scientists, and participate in research symposiums. To be accepted into the DAPCEP, students need to have an interest in mathematics and science, have a minimum grade of at least a C+, and have a recommendation from a teacher or counselor.

Although there are no recent data on the efficacy of the DAPCEP, in 1990, Hill sent a survey to 3,170 students who participated in the program from 1976 to 1986. Of that number, 584 people returned the survey. The results revealed that 74 percent of DAPCEP alumni who were enrolled in college were majoring in a STEM-related field, and an impressive 81 percent of DAPCEP alumni who were college graduates attained a degree in STEM.

SAY YES DEMONSTRATION SCHOOLS PROJECT

The Say Yes to a Youngster's Future program was implemented to increase the interest and academic success of Black students in STEM education (Beane, 1990). This program emerged in 1987 with financial support from the Shell Company Foundation and the National Urban Coalition's Schools Project. The goals of the Say Yes Program include improving the confidence and competencies of teachers in mathematics and science, increasing the mathematics and science competencies and interests of minority elementary school students, facilitating the involvement of parents and communities in mathematics and science education, and increasing the skill level of racial and ethnic minority students in mathematics and science so they will be prepared for advanced level mathematics and science work beyond secondary school.

The Say Yes Program initially started as a two-year pilot program in the District of Columbia, but it has been implemented in schools in Houston and New Orleans as well. To determine whether schools can participate, they must meet the following criteria: an enrollment of at least 75 percent of Black and Hispanic students, underachieving students per their scores on standardized tests in mathematics and science, and a strong commitment from the school's principal and a team of teachers. Four critical elements comprise the Say Yes Program:

1. **School-Based Teams**: These are comprised of a small group of teachers and the principal. Essentially, the teams are charged with participating in the staff development activities, as well as the planning and implementation of the project at the school level.

2. **Staff Development**: Using test score data and classroom observations, the school district mathematics and science coordinators work closely with the school-based team to identify areas in the curriculum that are in need of improvement at the elementary school level. School teams participate in summer programs and in-service programs during the school year where they receive training from master secondary teachers in science and mathematics to develop greater competency with the areas identified as weak in the curriculum. Additional training includes Say Yes Family Math, which helps provide the school team with the appropriate philosophy and structure for involving parents in informal school-focused mathematics activities.

3. **Saturday Family Math and Science**: Although the times that sessions are offered varies across school districts, they are typically held once a month during the school year. Some sessions are held at the school, and others take place at community-based facilities (e.g., zoos, museums, nature centers) and last from two to three hours. Topics include explorations of electricity, chemistry, simple machines, light, weather, flight, fossils, insects, animal behavior, plants, and astronomy. Families work in concert with teachers and students by using activity sheets and instructional material. Spanish translations of the instructional forms are provided for Hispanic families with limited English proficiency. Families also leave the session with activities to try at home with the proper instructional materials needed to do so.

4. **Outreach**: To build community support for science and mathematics education, the Say Yes Program employs a variety of approaches (e.g., conferences, actively distributing information about Saturday Family Math and Science program, distributing T-shirts, and other special events). Efforts to build

community support include schools, representatives from the business sector, political leaders, parents, and community-based organizations. The purpose of this support is to raise awareness within the local community about Say Yes and its initiatives.

Research indicates that the Say Yes Program has a positive impact on students' academic performance in mathematics and science. Specifically, using data from students who took the Metropolitan Achievement Test (MAT) in spring of 1987 as a pretest and spring of 1988, the results revealed the following:

- The students of teachers participating in Say Yes made a 28.95 point gain, which is equivalent to a 1.2 grade increase in mathematics among participants, compared to an 18.56 point gain among students in the control classrooms.
- In reading, the students of teachers participating in Say Yes gained 28.52 points (a 0.7 grade equivalent), while students in the control classrooms gained 15.97 points (a 0.4 grade equivalent). Furthermore, students participating in the Saturday Math Program scored higher on the MAT in mathematics and reading compared with the control group. Specifically, participants gained 25.97 points in mathematics on the MAT, whereas nonparticipants gained 15.65 points, which is equivalent to a 1.1 grade increase for participants versus a 0.7 increase for nonparticipants. Participating students also gained 25.00 points (a 0.5 grade equivalent gain) in reading on the MAT, whereas nonparticipants gained 12.24 points (a 0.4 grade equivalent gain).

THE STEM INSTITUTE

The STEM Institute is an initiative at the K–12 level to help increase the success of minority students in STEM. The STEM Institute is a collaborative initiative between various programs at the City College of New York (The STEM Institute, n.d.). The program, which functions as a summer academic enrichment program, was founded in 1992 and aims to help minority students in grade 9–11 increase their academic potential by providing them with early exposure to college work. In addition to academic support, it also offers students tutorial support. Specifically, the STEM Institute offers courses in the physical sciences, mathematics, English, engineering, and computer programming. A select group of students is also offered the opportunity to conduct research with faculty at the Grove School of Engineering.

The STEM institute is free, and eligibility is based on a multitude of factors. For one, students must demonstrate a commitment to succeed in science, engineering, or mathematics. Students must also have a high school average of 90 percent, and their Regents scores in math and science must be 90 percent or better. In addition, students must have a record of good attendance and display a willingness to participate in different aspects of the program until they graduate from high school.

Finally, they must also promise to maintain contact with the program while enrolled in college. Students who are accepted into the STEM Institute will receive free textbooks and other supplies. They will also be provided with breakfast and lunch.

Engineering, science, and mathematics faculty at the City College of New York and high school educators teach students who participate in the STEM Institute. Student participants also interact and receive visits from scientists and engineers working with different corporations. These individuals talk to the students about the various career options available in engineering and other science-related disciplines. In addition to these aspects, the parents of student participants are encouraged to be actively engaged in this program. Specifically, the program holds a parent-student orientation before each program begins in the summer to discuss the roles and responsibilities of both parties. Finally, student participants in the STEM Institute also take part in information sessions regarding the college application process, scholarships, and other college-related resources. Unlike the previous three programs highlighted, there is no data to gauge the efficacy of this initiative. Nevertheless, the STEM Institute does offer promising insight into various factors that could be useful in helping to facilitate the success of Black students in STEM.

THE TECH APPRENTICE PROGRAM

The Tech Apprentice Program was created to promote the success of Black students in STEM (Tech Apprentice Program, n.d.). The Tech Apprentice Program works collaboratively with both public and private industry, such as TechBoston, Boston Public Schools, Boston Private Industry Council, and the BPS Office of Instructional and Information Technology. The Tech Apprentice Program provides a seven-week internship opportunity at local companies for technology-oriented high school students in Boston. Students participating in this internship experience typically have an interest in pursuing an IT major in college, and the internship provides work experience to help them understand the diverse options available in the high-tech arena.

Since its implementation in the summer of 2006, more than 50 Boston-area companies have participated in this initiative, and more than 570 high school students have been placed in IT internships. These interns work in a variety of areas, such as financial services, health care, nonprofit, higher education, media, and IT. From software programmers to videographers, a large number of high school students from the Boston Public School system have spent their summers working as tech interns. Experiences and skills gained from this endeavor have contributed to their talent and enabled them to learn new skills that will be critical as they select a college major in IT and gain additional professional work experience in this field. Although we were not able to find data to gauge the efficacy of this initiative, we were able to find a video that discusses Tech Apprentice success stories. Visit this Web site to learn more about their stories: http://www.bostonpublicschools.org/Page/5674.

METRO EARLY COLLEGE HIGH SCHOOL

Metro Early College High School (hereafter referred to as Metro) was established in 2006 because The Ohio State University and Battelle Memorial Institute desired to create a "small" STEM school with "a big footprint" (Metro Early College High School, n.d.). With this in mind, Metro functions as a partnership among the high school, businesses, and the K–12 system. In addition to the high school, there is also a Metro Early Middle School and a Metro Institute of Technology. These are relatively new additions to the Metro educational system, with the Metro Middle School opening in the fall of 2013 and Metro Institute of Technology opening in the fall of 2015.

Metro strives to provide its students with a personalized intellectual environment that connects them to a world where math and science are important. Metro employs a holistic approach to educate its students, which is undergirded by a mission that involves six core components: effective communication, active learning, active and responsible decision-making, team work, critical thinking, and authentic engagement. Ten Common Principles of the Coalition of Essential Schools also guide the school. These principles are inspiring high schools across the nation to rethink their approach and philosophy as it relates to the way they educate their students. According to Metro Early College High School (n.d.), the principles are as follows:

1. The school's central intellectual purpose is helping students to use their minds well.
2. An essential body of knowledge, skills, and dispositions will be identified for student mastery.
3. The school's goals apply to all students.
4. The school will be highly personalized.
5. A governing practical metaphor will be "student-as-worker, teacher-as-coach."
6. Teaching and learning will be documented by student performance on real tasks.
7. The tone of the school will be trust and decency.
8. The principal and teachers will act as generalists first and specialists second.
9. Resources will be modest and therefore positioned toward teaching and learning.
10. The school will emphasize democratic, fair, and equitable practices.

Admission to Metro is nonselective. Students from across the state of Ohio can apply, and admission is determined by a lottery system. Potential students are also given the opportunity to interview with current faculty, students, and families of Metro to determine if the school is a good fit. The Metro curriculum is divided into two phases: college prep and college access. The college prep component occurs during the students' 9th and 10th year and includes students engaging in courses such as mathematics, science, social studies, and language arts. In addition to these courses, students also engage in challenges designed to investigate their solutions to real-world problems. These challenges highlight students' ability to work both independently and with others. Upon mastering the college prep phase of the curriculum, students move into the college access aspect of the curriculum where they engage in nontraditional learning tactics. For example, they experience educational practices that emphasize learning outside the classroom setting. In this regard, students take courses at the learning center and take college courses at either The Ohio State University or Columbus State University. They also participate in an internship. The kinds of courses students enroll in are dictated by their interest. Whereas the college prep curriculum emphasizes capacity building, the college access part of the curriculum places emphasis on skill development, social maturity, practical experiences, critical thinking, and responsibility.

Although there is no official data on the efficacy of Metro's impact on increasing the access of minority students in STEM in general and Black students specifically, there is an attempt to collect such data. Specifically, researchers from The George Washington University are conducting the Opportunity Structure for Preparation and Inspiration in STEM study to determine what makes STEM high schools, such as Metro, successful (Lynch, 2015). In addition to Metro, seven other schools are included in this study:

- Manor New Technology High School, Manor, TX
- Wayne School of Engineering, Goldsboro, NC
- Dozier-Libbey Medical High School, Antioch, CA
- Gary and Jerri-Ann Jacobs High Tech High Charter School, San Diego, CA
- Chicago High School for Agricultural Sciences, Chicago, IL
- Denver School of Science and Technology: Stapleton High School, Denver, CO
- Urban Science Academy, West Roxbury, MA

The researchers selected these STEM preparatory schools, which ranged from public to private charter schools, based on several factors, including the enrollment of a high proportion of minority students, recommendations from experts, high-standardized test scores, strong attendance records, and high graduate rates. Early findings from their study have shown that several factors across the schools contribute to the uniqueness and success of schools such as Metro. For example, the researchers cited the "broad and deep curriculum designed for all students with little tracking or ability group," as important to these schools (Lynch, 2015). They explained that this ensured all students receive the same level of high-quality learning experiences in all classes. They also discovered that schools such as Metro had teaching staff with advanced content knowledge. Lynch (2015) also indicated that all schools contained "a mission-focused administrative structure with flattened hierarchy that invited collaboration with and among teachers and students."

The researchers also noted that these schools provided support for minority students that came in the form of advisories to help students with personalized college planning, summer research programs on college campuses, and tutorial support. A positive school culture, defined by rituals and traditions that acknowledge and celebrate student accomplishments, teacher innovation, parental commitment, and a shared ethos of caring and concern for student achievement also contribute to the success of schools such as Metro. In addition, dynamic, personalized assessment systems, emphasis on real-world experience, and fostering opportunities of learning that develop initiative, self-regulation, persistence, and collaboration were other important factors that contribute to the uniqueness and success of such schools.

According to Lynch (2015):

STEM-focused high schools are important because they constitute the first U.S. science and mathematics reform that requires whole-school transformation rather than tinkering with peripheral components of an outmoded education system or serving just a small, select segment of the public school population. The advent of ISHSs [STEM-focused schools] is exciting because they not only provide access to students underserved by the current education system but also find ways to *support* these students in ways that traditional schools often do not. High school students need not just a rigorous course of study to prepare them for college majors but also meaningful encounters with the world of work that can reveal the range of possibilities open to them. They need a clear view of college pathways and how to navigate them, including financial aid. They need firsthand experiences with researchers and opportunities to interact with professionals in order to develop skills, confidence, and social capital. Equally important, the U.S. and other countries need such changes in their systems of education to make opportunities more widely available to all, and change notions about who "does" STEM. In this way we can help solve the twin problems of increasing the number of qualified professionals while shrinking the social mobility and income gaps that threaten to upend our economies and the nature of our social system.

AP STEM ACCESS PROGRAM

The AP (Advanced Placement) STEM Access Program was created in 2013 to increase the number of traditionally underrepresented minorities and female high school students who participate in advanced placement courses in STEM disciplines (AP STEM Access Program, n.d.). This program was made possible due to a $5 million grant from Google as part of its Global Impact Award, which enabled more than 320 public high schools to start more than 500 new AP courses in such subjects as math, science, and computer science. Part of this funding also covered classroom resources, educational resources, and professional development for teachers. Participating schools must agree to maintain the new courses for a minimum of three years. To be eligible to participate in this initiative, schools must have the following characteristics:

* Be a public school
* Have a high population of underrepresented students who are academically prepared for rigorous coursework in AP STEM classes as dictated by their scores on the Preliminary SAT/National Merit Scholarship Qualified Test
* Be situated in communities with a median household income of $100,000 or less and/or have 40 percent or more students qualifying for free and reduced school lunch

Similar to the STEM Institute, the Tech Apprentice Program, and the Metro Early College High School Program, there is no data to assess the effectiveness of this initiative. Given that the program was recently implemented in 2013, the lack of data gauging its efficacy is not surprising. Nevertheless, we thought it was important to include this program because it does add additional context on actionable programs that have been created to increase the participation and success of Black students in STEM.

Given that the preceding section has critically reviewed and provided context on the seven programmatic initiatives implemented at the K–12 level to increase the access, participation, and success of Black students in STEM, Table 2.1 summarizes those initiatives and highlights their core components.

Table 2.1   Programmatic Initiatives at the K–12 Level to Help Facilitate the Preparedness of Black Students in STEM

Programs	Objectives
Pre-Engineering Program at the University of Akron	This program functions as an after-school and summer program that helps to increase the preparedness of Blacks and other minorities in STEM. Students in grades 9–12 can participate in this program, but they must be residents of Ohio, Pennsylvania, Indiana, and Michigan. In addition to the academic components, this program also features a series of career workshops and provides students tutorial support throughout the school year.
Detroit Area Pre-College Engineering Program	Implement in 1976 with a grant from the Alfred P. Sloan Foundation, the Detroit Area Pre-College Engineering Program works with the Detroit Public School System and local universities, corporations, and businesses to increase the number of middle and high school students in general and minority students specifically who pursue careers in STEM. To do this, the program offers Saturday classes, a summer academic program, and classes in pre-engineering and science, which are held at public schools in Detroit.

(*continued*)

Table 2.1   (*Continued*)

Programs	Objectives
Say Yes Demonstration Schools Project	Created in 1987, this program aims to increase the participation and success of minorities in STEM via four objectives: (1) improving the competencies of teachers in mathematics and science, (2) increasing the mathematics and science competencies and interests of students in elementary schools, (3) involving parents in the students' educational process, and (4) increasing the skill level of minorities in mathematics and science
The STEM Institute	This summer academic program is housed at the City College of New York for students in grades 9–11 to help them increase their preparedness and success for STEM majors at the college level.
The Tech Apprentice Program	The Tech Apprentice Program works in tandem with public and private entities in Boston to help increase the skill set of high school students in STEM. One of the critical ways they do this is by providing students with internship opportunities in IT industries.
Metro Early College High School	This initiative in Ohio is a high school that places a special purpose on increasing the success of students in general and minorities specifically in STEM. Admission to Metro is nonselective and is determined by a lottery system. Additional measures, such as interviews with faculty and current students helps to ensure a good fit. The Metro curriculum is divided into two components and functions to prepare students for success in college, particularly in STEM fields.
AP STEM Access Program	This is a relatively new initiative, created in 2013, with a grant, in part, from Google, to increase the number of underrepresented high school students and female students who participate in advanced placement courses in STEM. Since its inception, this program has afforded more than 320 public high schools to start more than 500 new AP courses in subjects such as mathematics, science, and computer science.

CONCLUDING THOUGHTS

This chapter has provided context on seven programs implemented at the K–12 level with the intent of increasing the participation and success of Blacks and other minorities in STEM at the college level. Although not all of these programs are supported by empirical evidence to help gauge their effectiveness, they all offer rich insight into practices and conditions that could be useful in helping to promote the achievement of Black students in STEM. Moreover, in Chapter One of this book, we emphasized the importance of academic preparations. Given that structural inequalities largely preclude Blacks and other underrepresented minorities from receiving appropriate and sufficient academic preparations, preparatory programs in STEM at the K–12 level can help to fill this gap.

In the third chapter of this book, *Financial Support for Black STEM Students*, we will discuss scholarship resources that Black students can use to help support their access and success as STEM majors in college.

NOTE

Portions of this chapter have been adapted from Museus, S. D., Palmer, R. T., Davis, R. J., & Maramba, D. C. (2011). *Racial and ethnic minority students' success in STEM education.* Hoboken, NJ: Jossey-Bass. Used by permission.

CHAPTER THREE

Financial Support for Black STEM Students

The success of Black STEM students is inextricably linked to their ability to pay for college. Several studies have found that financial factors are critical to the retention of Black students in STEM (e.g., Museus, Palmer, Davis, & Maramba, 2011; Maton & Hrabowski, 2004; May & Chubin, 2003; Seymour & Hewitt, 1997). For example, Seymour and Hewitt conducted a study that included individual interviews and focus groups with approximately 460 minority students and found that lack of financial support was one of the most salient reasons for their higher attrition in STEM fields than their White counterparts. Seymour and Hewitt's findings are not shocking given that Black, Hispanic, and Native American students are more likely to come from low economic backgrounds compared to their White peers.

Several trends emphasize the importance of considering students' ability to pay for higher education and its impact on their success in STEM. First, given the continuously rising tuition rates and increased reliance on loans in the composition of financial aid packages, it is unlikely that threats to Black college students' ability to pay will subside. Second, evidence suggests that students in STEM are more likely to be awarded scholarships based on merit than need (e.g., Fenske, Porter, & DuBrock, 2000; Museus et al., 2011). Given that Black students are more likely to be insufficiently prepared for STEM majors, the allocation of resources to fund merit-based, rather than need-based, aid can also negatively impact their ability to pay. In the following sections, we discuss three financial factors that affect the ability of Black students in STEM to pay for college: college costs, financial aid, and employment.

THE IMPACT OF COLLEGE COSTS

College costs have been rising significantly for the past two decades. The average annual tuition and fees required to attend a public four-year institution for the

2015–2016 academic year are $9,410 for in-state students and $23,893 for out-of-state students, but that number is $32,405 for those attending private four-year campuses (Collegedata, n.d.). Moreover, because college costs are rising faster than average family income, an increasing number of students have unmet financial need and greater difficulties paying for college. Two major ways that Black students in STEM deal with the increasing costs of postsecondary education are by using financial aid awards and working.

THE ROLE OF FINANCIAL AID AWARDS

Research indicates that financial aid influences success among Black students in STEM, but this relationship is unclear. For example, research show that some types of financial aid have a positive influence, whereas others have a questionable impact. Financial aid awards in general are positively related to success for minority students in engineering. Specifically, gifts in the form of scholarships and grants have been linked to higher rates of persistence and degree attainment for minority students. Given that low-income students in STEM are less likely to complete college degrees, access to financial aid, especially grants, is vital for these students.

According to the General Accounting Office (1995), "The influence of loans appears to be more complex, with researchers finding loan amounts to be both positively and negatively correlated with success. While more research is needed to make sense of these conflicting results, what is clear is that loans appear to facilitate success among White students more effectively than Black students." This finding could be due to the fact that Black students are more sensitive to college costs and more averse to taking out loans to finance their college education. Regardless of the reason, the fact that loans might not be as likely to increase success among Black students in STEM is interesting, given that policy makers have increasingly relied on loans in the composition of financial aid packages.

THE IMPACT OF EMPLOYMENT

Employment has been shown to influence success among Black students in STEM, but that impact depends on the location and nature of work. Generally, research shows that working off campus is negatively associated with success, especially working more than 25 hours per week off campus (Museus et al., 2011). Conversely, research indicates that working on campus can positively influence success (e.g., Kuh, Kinzie, Buckley, Bridges, & Hayek, 2007). Finally, there is some indication that working on a research project with professors is positively associated with success among minorities in STEM (Hurtado et al., 2007), but by and large the impact of specific kinds of work on success has not been the focus of empirical inquiry.

Inability to pay for college or insufficient financial resources, however, can force Black students in STEM, as well as other majors, to work a substantial number of hours to pay for their expenses, thereby negatively affecting their likelihood of success. Researchers have revealed that, due to inadequate finances, many minority students in general and in STEM need to have a job to compensate for their school and living expenses (Palmer, Davis, & Hilton, 2009). The pressure to work to compensate for financial struggles can disproportionately hinder success among minority students. For example, Hispanics who encounter financial concerns often find jobs that hinder their academic performance in STEM courses. In addition, Hispanic students are more likely than other racial groups to work longer hours, which has been associated with their leaving college. Nevertheless, it is likely that low-income Black and Native American students in STEM are also likely to work long hours and suffer negative consequences on their success. In sum, the ability to pay for college is a major factor influencing the success of Black students in STEM. Rising college costs, trends toward increased reliance on loans in the composition of financial aid packages, and the emphasis on merit-based aid in STEM fields might all contribute to financial pressures for Black students to be successful in STEM.

In light of this information, this chapter focuses on forms of financial support to help Black students in STEM majors in higher education. Research reveals that a number of financial resources are available to help the retention and persistence of Black students in STEM. Given that the literature reviewed has demonstrated a positive relationship between scholarships and the retention and persistence of Black students in STEM, we specifically focus on scholarships to help support the access and success of Black students. This chapter delineates these scholarships by exploring an overview of their purpose, discussing the eligibility requirements, and providing relevant contact information.

FINANCIAL RESOURCES TO HELP SUPPORT THE ACCESS, PARTICIPATION, AND SUCCESS OF BLACK STEM STUDENTS IN HIGHER EDUCATION

Through a search of Web sites, we have identified several scholarships to help support the success of students in STEM. Many of the scholarships are specifically focused on Black students. This chapter focuses on the following scholarships:

- Microsoft Scholarship
- National Society of Black Engineers Scholarship
- Buick Achievers Scholarship
- VIP Women in Technology Scholarship (WITS)
- Xerox Technical Minority Scholarship
- United Negro College Fund (UNCF) STEM Scholarship
- Gates Millennium Scholars (GMS)
- National Action Council for Minorities in Engineering Scholarship

- Development Fund for Black Students in Science and Technology Scholarship
- UNCF/Merck Undergraduate Science Research Scholarship Awards
- Society of Women Engineering Scholarship

This chapter provides an overview for each scholarship, including its mission, eligibility criteria, and contact information. To conclude the chapter, a brief summary of the key themes is presented.

Microsoft Scholarship

Microsoft awards tuition scholarships each year to encourage students to enter computer science and other related fields in STEM. Students are selected for the scholarship based on their passion for technology, academic excellence, and leadership potential. Although this scholarship is open to all students, Microsoft is intentional about diversifying the STEM field. To this end, they have awarded a large number of scholarships to female students and underrepresented minorities, such as Hispanics, Blacks, Native Americans, and students with disabilities. In addition to providing support with tuition, recipients of this scholarship will participate in technical conferences, such as Grace Hopper Celebration of Women in Computing, Society of Hispanic Professional Engineers (SHPE), and National Society of Black Engineers (NSBE), among others. The scholarship covers the cost of conference registration, assists with travel costs, and contributes to other related expenses. This scholarship is only available to students already enrolled in a four-year postsecondary institution. Therefore, students who are in high school or enrolled in a community college are ineligible. Students who want to learn more about this and other Microsoft-related scholarships can e-mail scholars@microsoft.com.

National Society of Black Engineers (NSBE)

The National Society of Black Engineers (NSBE) offers a wide array of corporate-sponsored scholarships to precollege students, undergraduates, graduate students, and technical professional members. Scholarships from NSBE range from $500 to $10,500. In addition to scholarships, the group also provides awards that acknowledge its highest achieving members. These awards, such as the Mike Shinn Distinguished Member of the Year Program or the Alumni Member and Technologist of the Year, include a cash award that ranges up to $7,500. To be eligible for any NSBE scholarship, students must be an active and paid NSBE member. Students must also submit their transcript for GPA confirmation to the World Headquarters. They can e-mail their transcripts to scholarships@nsbe.org.

NSBE rules indicate that recipients of scholarships cannot be awarded more than two scholarships in a given year. Members that apply for more than one scholarship that has an internship requirement must decide which scholarship/internship they want to accept in priority order before selection because a member cannot accept both internships for a given time period. Students can find out more about NSBE and its scholarships at http://www.nsbe.org.

Buick Achievers Scholarship

The Buick Achievers Scholarship provides financial assistance for students who have succeeded in and outside the classroom. This scholarship is particularly geared toward students who may not be able to attend college without financial assistance. The impetus for this scholarship is to reward students for their hard work and tenacity and the difference they have made in the lives of others. The Buick Achievers Scholarship provides up to $25,000 per year for 50 first-time freshmen or students already enrolled in college. This scholarship is renewable for up to five years. The Buick Achievers Scholarship is funded by the General Motors Foundation, which is credited for donating millions of dollars to educational organizations and disaster relief efforts since 1976.

Students applying for the Buick Achievers Scholarship must have the following qualifications:

- Be a high school senior, high school graduate, or current college student
- Plan to enroll in a full-time undergraduate study at an accredited four-year college
- Plan to major in a specific field related to STEM or a business-related program of study
- Demonstrate an interest in pursuing a career in the automotive or related industries after completing college
- Be a U.S. citizen and have permanent residence in the United States or Puerto Rico

The award criteria for the Buick Achievers Scholarship include the following:

- Academic achievement and financial need
- Participation and leadership in the community and school activities
- Work experience and interest in pursuing a career in the automotive or related industries

Special consideration will be given to first-generation college students, females, minorities, military veterans, and dependents of military personnel.
To learn more about the Buick Achievers Scholarship, students can visit http://www.buickachievers.com.

VIP Women in Technology Scholarship (WITS) Program

The VIP Women in Technology, which is a program sponsored by the Visionary Integration Professionals (VIP), has a scholarship opportunity for students. The

Women in Technology Scholarship (WITS) is awarded annually to women across the United States. To be eligible for WITS, students must be enrolled or accepted in a two- or four-year college in the United States. Students must also be planning on pursuing a career in computer science, information technology, management information systems, computer engineering, or another related field. The Women in Technology program grants multiple scholarships that range up to $2,500. The following evaluation criteria are used for the award:

• Students must show academic performance with a GPA of 3.0 or higher.
• Students must respond thoughtfully to questions on an essay exam.
• Students must actively participate in community service and extracurricular activities.

For more information about WITS, students can e-mail WITS@trustvip.com.

Xerox Technical Minority Scholarship

Xerox offers Technical Minority Scholarships to students in STEM, but unlike WITS, the scholarships from Xerox are not gender specific. Moreover, the Xerox Technical Minority Scholarships are particularly focused on minority students in engineering. Eligibility includes being a full-time student at a four-year college or university; having at least a B average or better; planning to graduate with a BS, MS, or PhD in a technical science or an engineering discipline; being of minority status; and demonstrating financial need. The award ranges from $1,000 to $10,000. Students can find out more about this scholarship by visiting http://www.xerox.com /en-us/jobs/minority-scholarships.

United Negro College Fund (UNCF) STEM Scholarship

The United Negro College Fund (UNCF) offers a scholarship to Black students in STEM. The UNCF STEM scholarship program is a 10-year initiative aimed at identifying and providing scholarships and academic support to approximately 500 Black high school students who aspire to earn degrees in STEM and subsequently enter the STEM field. Specifically, this scholarship will enable students to pursue studies in STEM at historically Black colleges and universities (HBCUs), private colleges, state and technical colleges, and universities.

The UNCF STEM scholarship provides up to $25,000 in scholarship tuition. Freshmen and sophomores are eligible to receive up to $2,500 per academic year, whereas juniors and seniors are eligible to receive up to $5,000. Scholarships are renewable for up to five years. Maintaining the scholarship entails earning a 2.5 GPA and being enrolled in a degree program on a full-time basis. Students who qualify to participate in the UNCF STEM scholarship program also receive academic support and mentoring, access to online support services, and other STEM-related support services. In addition, they participate in a K–12 STEM Summer Institute, which is a pre-college workshop; attend a UNCF Student Tech Empowerment Workshop, and receive career-development support.

The following are the eligibility requirements for the UNCF STEM scholarship:

- Being Black
- Being a U.S. Citizen
- Having a cumulative high school GPA of 3.0 and pursuing an intense course of study in high school
- Having a demonstrated financial need
- Demonstrating readiness and a commitment to pursue STEM majors, including biological life sciences, physics, chemistry, computer science, engineering, information sciences, and mathematics
- Completing all of the application essays
- Arranging for letters of recommendations to be submitted
- Being enrolled as a first-time student at an accredited institution of higher education in the United States
- Completing and submitting the application by the deadline

To enhance the chances of earning the scholarship, UNCF encourages applicants to have conversations with teachers, counselors, and parents about what is required to be a strong candidate for college admission and student aid. They recommended that applicants carefully consider which teachers and STEM program sponsors to ask for a letter of recommendation. They also encourage students to complete the Free Application for Federal Student Aid (FAFSA) before they apply for the scholarship. If students are selected as finalists for the scholarship, the FAFSA will be used to confirm their citizenship and understand their financial need. UNCF also advise students to review their transcript so they can be sure their GPA and the courses they have taken make them eligible for the program. Finally, they ask students to let them know about their interests, goals, motivation, and experience that have shaped their decision to pursue an undergraduate degree in STEM. Students can find out more about the UNCF STEM Scholarship from the following Web site: https://scholarships.uncf.org.

Gates Millennium Scholars (GMS)

The Bill and Melinda Gates Foundation funds the Gates Millennium Scholars (GMS) program, which is administered by the UNCF. The purpose of GMS is to support the cost of education for undergraduate students in any academic discipline. Students can also apply for the scholarship if they plan to attend graduate school and have unmet needs. The scholarship provides support to graduate students in the following academic areas: computer science, education, engineering, library science, mathematics, public health, or science.

Similar to some of the previous scholarships discussed in this chapter, the purpose of GMS is to increase the economic competitiveness of the United States by enhancing the preparedness of minority students in STEM. A student interested in applying for GMS must be a U.S. citizen, have a cumulative high school GPA of 3.3, matriculate into an accredited college or university, demonstrate leadership activities through participation in community service or extracurricular activities, meet the federal Pell Grant eligibility criteria, and complete and submit the following forms: the application, an evaluation of the student's academic record, and an evaluation of the student's community service and leadership activities.

In addition to receiving financial support, students who are selected for GMS receive academic services that encourage academic excellence and receive mentoring services for academic and personal development. Finally, they are given access to an online resource center that provides information about internships, fellowships, and scholarships. To find more about GMS, students can visit http://www.gmsp.org.

National Action Council for Minorities in Engineering (NACME) Scholarship

The National Action Council for Minorities in Engineering (NACME) provides another scholarship opportunity to Black students in STEM. Similar to some of the other scholarship providers (e.g., GMS), the goal of NACME is to help increase the competitiveness of the United States in the global marketplace by increasing the preparedness of minority students in STEM. NACME has awarded more than $4 million in scholarships to minority students. In 2016, NACME anticipates awarding scholarships to more than 1,300 students in engineering.

NACME provides block grants to postsecondary education institutions, which, in turn, award the money to deserving students as part of their financial aid package. NACME or the universities that NACME has established partnerships with identify eligible students for this scholarship. To qualify, students must fall into one of three categories: a first-year student, a transfer student from a two-year college, or currently enrolled in a university with at least one year of course study in engineering completed. Universities interested in partnership with NACME must demonstrate a commitment to the recruitment, admission, retention, education, and graduation rates of minority students. Moreover, students desiring to receive a scholarship from NACME must enroll in an engineering program at a university in which NACME has established a partnership. Students must also be classified as minorities and maintain a minimum GPA from 2.5 to 2.8.

Recall that students who are eligible for the NACME scholarship must fall into one of three categories: first-year college student, transfer student from a two-year institution, or completed one year of course study in engineering at the university level. Eligibility requirements for the NACME scholarship are dictated by the category the students fall in. For example, first-year students must have a high school GPA of at least a 2.5 and be accepted into a college or university engineering program by the end of their freshmen year. In addition, students who are currently enrolled in the university must have completed a calculus, physics, or chemistry course with a letter grade of at least a B and be accepted into an engineering program. Finally, community college transfers must enter into a four-year university as third-year engineering students with a 2.7 cumulative GPA. To learn more about this scholarship, students can visit http://www.nacme.org.

Development Fund for Black Students in Science and Technology (DFBSST)

The Development Fund for Black Students in Science and Technology (DFBSST) is an endowment that provides scholarships to Black students in the STEM fields at HBCUs. Since its inception in 1983, DFBSTT has awarded more than $385,000 in scholarships to more than 149 students who have pursued an education in the STEM fields. Out of the 149 students, 130 students have already graduated, and several recipients of the DFBSTT scholarships have earned PhDs in fields such as engineering and astronomy. Students are identified for the DFBSST scholarship through science and engineering deans and professors at preselected HBCUs. Once identified, deans and professors will distribute a form to the students with information about the DFBSST scholarship. To be eligible for a scholarship from DFBSST, a student must be a Black undergraduate majoring in a STEM field. They must also be enrolled at a qualifying HBCU.[1]

Students' applications are evaluated on the following criteria after they apply for the DFBSST scholarship: grades and SAT scores, especially in math and science; responses to personal essays; descriptions of career goals and extracurricular activities; letters of recommendation; and financial need. The DFBSST scholarship committee determines the amount of financial aid selected students will receive. Typically, students are awarded up to $2,000 per year. This scholarship is renewable for up to four years as long as the student remains in good academic standing, maintains at least a 3.0 in their major (e.g., science or engineering), and is enrolled as a full-time, undergraduate student. Students can find more information about the scholarship by visiting http://www.dfbsstscholarship.org/dfb_prg.html.

UNCF/Merck Undergraduate Science Research Scholarship Awards

The United Negro College Fund and the Merck Company have formed a partnership to help increase the number of Black students majoring and working in the biomedical field. At least 15 students are selected per year for the UNCF/Merck Scholarship. Eligibility for this scholarship includes being a Black student, being a permanent citizen of the United States, having a minimum GPA of 3.3 or above, and majoring in physical science or engineering.[2]

Recipients of the UNCF-Merck Scholarship are awarded up to $25,000 in tuition, room and board, and billable fees. Aside from the financial support, each scholarship recipient is recognized as a UNCF/Merck fellow, is mentored by a scientist, and may receive a summer internship. The selection committee for the scholarship consists of educators, scientists, and engineers. Students are selected for the UNCF/Merck Scholarship based on their GPA, their interest in furthering their scientific education and pursuing a career in science research, and their interest and ability in performing laboratory work. Students can find out more about the scholarship by visiting http://umsi.uncf.org/sif.

Society of Women in Engineering Scholarship

Society of Women in Engineering (SWE) provides financial support to women in accredited baccalaureate and graduate programs in engineering, engineering technology, and computer science. In 2015, SWE awarded 220 scholarships, totaling over $660,000. Scholarships are awarded in May for sophomores, juniors, seniors, and graduate students and in June for freshmen and reentry students.[3] With this scholarship, students may be awarded $1,000 to $15,000 in financial support. Although there is no GPA requirement for freshmen and reentering students, it is not quite clear what the GPA requirement is for students in other academic standings (e.g., sophomores, juniors, seniors, and graduate students). Students can find out more about this scholarship by visiting http://societyofwomenengineers.swe.org/swe-scholarships.

This chapter provided an overview of scholarships for Black students in STEM. In addition to the overview, this chapter also discussed eligibility requirements and funding amounts. Table 3.1 summarizes the scholarship information discussed in the preceding section of this chapter.

CONCLUDING THOUGHTS

Research suggests that one of the primary ways to support the success of Black students in STEM in higher education is through grants and scholarships. With this in mind, this chapter reviewed a variety of scholarships to gain an understanding of the resources available to support the success of Black students in STEM in higher education. In this chapter, we discussed 11 scholarships aimed to help increase the access, participation, and success of students in STEM. Many of these scholarships are specifically focused on minority students. We strongly urge students to use the contact information provided to learn more about the scholarships discussed in this volume and to become more informed about deadline submission for these opportunities. Contacting these sources is also important because this chapter provided laconic information on these funding opportunities. Moreover, by contacting these organizations, this will potentially help students become informed about other sources for scholarships and other forms of financial support, as this chapter does not claim to provide an exhaustive overview of all funding support for Black students in STEM.

Table 3.1 Overview of Financial Support for Black STEM Students

Scholarships	Mission	Eligibility	Web Sites
Microsoft Scholarship	Scholarship is open to all students, but it functions to diversify the STEM field.	• Being a U.S. citizen • Being enrolled in a four-year college or university	https://careers.microsoft.com /students/scholarships
National Society of Black Engineers Scholarship	Scholarship aims to increase the number of Black students in the engineering field.	• Being an active NSBE member	http://www.nsbe.org
Buick Achievers Scholarship	Scholarship provides financial support for all students who demonstrate financial need.	• Being a current college student • Planning to enroll in college as a full-time student • Demonstrating an interest in pursuing a career in the automotive or related industries	http://www.buickachievers .com
VIP Women in Technology Scholarship (WITS)	Scholarship is for women in the STEM field.	• Being a woman • Having a cumulative GPA of 3.0 or above • Responding to an essay question • Actively participating in community service or extracurricular activities	http://www.trustvip.com/news /press-releases/vip-announces -2016-women-in-technology -scholarship-wits-program/
Xerox Technical Minority Scholarship	Scholarship is focused on diversifying the STEM field.	• Being a full-time student at a four-year institution • Having at least a B average or better • Planning to graduate with a degree in STEM • Being a minority student • Demonstrating financial need	http://www.xerox.com/jobs /minority-scholarships/enus .html

(continued)

39

Table 3.1 (*Continued*)

Scholarships	Mission	Eligibility	Web Sites
United Negro College Fund STEM Scholarship	Scholarship provides academic and scholarly support to Black high school students interested in STEM.	• Having a cumulative high school GPA of 3.0 or above • Demonstrating financial need • Demonstrating a commitment to pursue STEM majors • Providing letters of recommendation	https://scholarships.uncf.org
Gates Millennium Scholars	Scholarship aims to diversity the STEM field.	• Being a minority from a prescribed background • Having a cumulative high school GPA of 3.3 • Matriculating into an accredited institution of higher education • Demonstrating leadership skills and abilities • Meeting the Pell Grant eligibility criteria	http://www.gmsp.org
National Action Council for Minorities in Engineering Scholarship	Scholarship aims to help students in the engineering field.	• Being a first year student • Transferring from a community college or currently enrolled in college with one year of completed coursework in engineering by the end of freshmen year	http://www.nacme.org

40

Scholarship	Description	Eligibility	URL
Development Fund for Black Students in Science and Technology Scholarship	Scholarship supports the success of Black students in STEM at HBCUs.	• Being a student enrolled in an HBCU that is supported by DFBSST • Majoring in the STEM field	http://www.dfbsstscholarship.org/dfb_prg.html
UNCF/Merck Undergrad Science Research Scholarship Awards	Scholarship aims to increase the representation of Black students in the biomedical science and research field.	• Majoring in the physical sciences or the engineering field • Desiring to be more engaged in research and laboratory work	http://umsi.uncf.org/sif
Society of Women in Engineering Scholarships	Scholarship aims to increase the number of women in the engineering field.	• Being a woman in the engineering field (freshmen, reentry, graduate students, and nontraditional students) • Attending accredited engineering programs	http://societyofwomen engineers.swe.org/swe -scholarships

41

In the next chapter of this book, *Surviving and Thriving in the First Year of College*, we discuss practical action steps Black STEM students can take early in their college career to succeed. The three action steps are choosing the right institution; following key student-level strategies, practices, and skills; and taking advantage of institutional support systems.

NOTES

1. Bennett College, Clark Atlanta University, Elizabeth City State University, Fisk University, Florida A&M University, Fort Valley State University, Hampton University, Howard University, Langston University, Lincoln University, Morehouse College, Morgan State University, North Carolina A&T State University, Prairie View A&M University, Spelman College, Southern University, Tennessee State University, Tuskegee University, Wilberforce University, and Xavier University of Louisiana

2. Aerospace engineering, agriculture, animal science, biochemistry, biological sciences, biology, biomedical engineering, biomedical research, chemical engineering, chemistry, comp biology, ecology, engineering, environmental engineering, environmental science(s), forestry, kinesiology, material science, mathematical sciences, mechanical engineering, medicine, microbiology, pharmacy, physical sciences, pre-medicine, pre-pharmacy, pre-vet, psychology, science, science technology.

3. Students who have been out of school for a minimum of two years prior to beginning their course of study are not eligible for this grant. Moreover, students who have been out of the engineering or technology workforce for a minimum of two years prior to the beginning of their course of study are not eligible for this grant as well.

CHAPTER FOUR

Surviving and Thriving in the First Year of College

The goal of this chapter is to help Black STEM students survive and thrive during the first year of college. Success is not an overnight accomplishment; it is a journey. If success were easy, every student would achieve it. The first year in college is a crucial time for establishing the foundational persistence, behaviors, and skills that will produce success throughout college and beyond.

To aid first-year students with laying this foundation, this chapter presents three concrete action steps that are supported by research and proven ingredients for a successful and enjoyable first year in college: (1) choosing the right institution; (2) following key student-level strategies, practices, and skills; and (3) taking advantage of institutional support systems. A section in this chapter is devoted to each step. We suggest that students spend a lot of time with this chapter and return to it regularly as a resource.

Students who take the right actions to guard against failure and pursue success will reap many long-term rewards. Even during the first year of college when many students are misusing their newfound freedom by living in the moment, keeping these long-term rewards in mind can help with motivation when difficulties and distractions arise. On a personal level, a successful student eventually will secure a satisfying career with the capacity to provide for self and family. In addition, the student will gain the opportunity and ability to create new knowledge, solve complex problems, and develop innovations that help real people. Not to be overlooked is the opportunity to contribute to societal progress. When one Black STEM student succeeds, all society moves forward. Given the persistent underrepresentation of Black Americans throughout the STEM marketplace, every new chemist, mathematician, physician, or holder of any other STEM job is a significant contribution toward the goal of full representation. Intractable problems such as race-based income and wealth inequality will only be solved when greater numbers of Blacks enter higher-paying careers. Furthermore, the entry of Blacks into fields where they are highly underrepresented can inspire and encourage others to pursue those fields because they are no longer considered "off limits." We have seen this phenomenon with the election of President Barack Obama, although the need for more everyday role models in all professions, including STEM, continues. These are just some of the rewards a student can expect to enjoy, and the foundation begins by taking the right actions early.

Before discussing the three action steps for first-year success in more detail, we should offer some additional thoughts about the special challenge of the first year. We will show how and why so much emphasis should be placed on the first year. After all, if a student fails in the first year, then any chance at ultimate success in a STEM career diminishes greatly.

THE SPECIAL CHALLENGE OF THE FIRST YEAR

We can begin with the basics. Depending on the language adopted by a particular college, students in their initial year are called first-year students or freshmen. Many are new high school graduates, and they are taking five classes plus a science lab. Added together, this typically equals 15 to 16 credit hours, and this number is important for a reason. Advisors often encourage students to register for at least five courses to promote on-time graduation within four years. Only in rare circumstances should students register for fewer than 15 credit hours—that is, three or four classes—because the inevitable result is delayed graduation. This is one of the first success tips that all incoming freshmen should follow: to graduate on time, register for a full load of courses. We discuss this in greater detail in Chapter Five.

Of course, attaining success in college requires more than registering for courses. Many students find the college experience new and exciting but also quite often intimidating and challenging. Although every year of college carries distinct trials, the initial year is especially pivotal. Pressures are so great that students of all races and ethnicities—not just Black students—are more likely to depart college during or immediately after their first year than any other. Understanding how to navigate this early period ahead of time will increase a student's chances of persisting to the end rather than dropping out. Given the challenges of this period and the lack of Black STEM degree holders, every effort to reinforce behaviors associated with first-year success can make a dramatic difference.

Whether students realize it or not, their college is highly aware of first-year challenges faced by their incoming students. In fact, institutions are judged (in part) by how many students reenroll from the freshman to sophomore year. This is known as the first-year retention rate. Every first-time, full-time freshman is included in this statistic, which is recorded and reported by all accredited institutions. According to the National Center for Education Statistics, the first-year retention rate is defined as the following:

... the rate at which students persist in their educational program at an institution, expressed as a percentage. For four-year institutions, this is the percentage of first-time bachelors (or equivalent) degree-seeking undergraduates from the previous fall who are again enrolled in the current fall.

The fact that the retention rate carries such a specific meaning for first-year students underscores the critical importance of this period in the life of a college student.

Retention rates for Black students are particularly concerning. One study compared rates across several races, finding that Black students were retained at 76.5 percent compared to Whites at 82 percent (Eagan & Alvarado, 2014). Moreover, research conducted by Berger and Milem (1999) suggested that being Black is "the third largest negative predictor of persistence" in college (p. 657; see also Harper, 2009). This is problematic because such early attrition from the college pipeline reduces the number of Black students even eligible to earn a STEM degree. Fewer degrees earned means fewer Blacks will enter STEM fields and enjoy the associated rewards.

To be clear, juxtaposing retention rates for Whites and Blacks should not give the impression that Blacks are inferior. The entire premise of this book is that Black students are equally capable of succeeding in STEM disciplines as other populations. What the lower retention rate among Black students might mean—and evidence detailed throughout this chapter suggests it does mean—is that institutions are better designed to promote the success of some student populations over others. Persistence challenges can be attributed to prejudicial or discriminatory systems that remain embedded in the space of higher education. Blacks can face additional barriers to success when compared with other populations such as Whites. These added barriers compound other barriers faced by all students to create extra-challenging circumstances that thwart larger numbers of Blacks from being retained and ultimately graduating. Therefore, students need to learn how to cross barriers, and institutions must reduce barriers. Responsibility belongs to all parties, as the remainder of this chapter will show through the three recommended action steps for first-year students.

ACTION STEP ONE: CHOOSING THE RIGHT INSTITUTION

Turning to the three action steps Black STEM students can take in their first year to promote success, the goal is to open a frank discussion of general success barriers and race-based success barriers. Some of these apply to all students, and some are more specific to Black students. We do not claim that all Black students experience every challenge or that they experience every challenge in the same way. However, we stress that proper preparation means being aware of the variety of challenges—both general and race-based—that a student might face to ensure they are not caught off guard. To this end, this chapter also provides practical strategies for navigating each challenge, beginning with which type of college to choose.

Choosing an institution is a monumental and challenging task for many students. Although this decision technically precedes a student's first year of college, we refer to it as the first action step for first-year student success because the two are connected. How a student experiences the first year of college after matriculating is determined in part by the institution the student selected. Although many other factors also determine the quality of the initial year, the place itself is foundational.

Another general reason to stress the importance of college choice is the high cost of transfer. Relocating to another school between a fall and spring semester or between academic years can be a stressful process. Even if a student's second institution is a better fit, the time invested at the first institution might come at a price. Transfer students often discover that some courses taken at a prior school will not follow them to the new school, which results in lost tuition, the possibility of accumulating more debt, and, worst of all, delayed graduation. For this and other reasons, choosing one's school carefully is a key variable in the success equation.

Because choosing a school carefully is an important first decision, a student must spend time learning about the options. To aid in this, we will discuss two broad types of institutions that Black STEM students are likely to consider: predominantly White institutions (PWIs) and historically Black colleges and universities (HBCUs). Although there are many ways to categorize institutions (e.g., selectivity, cost, Carnegie Classification), we will use the PWI-HBCU distinction in this book for two reasons. First, the distinction is a common one, so introducing it is an essential part of gaining a working knowledge of available options. Second, broad differences between PWIs and HBCUs offer a way of shedding light on many factors deemed important by Black college students, especially related to the impact of race and culture on higher education. This discussion will provide Black STEM students with clear, honest insight into an array of challenges and opportunities they face in pursuit of success. We will compare and contrast PWIs and HBCUs frequently throughout the remainder of this book so readers can become familiar with them.

Predominantly White Institutions (PWIs)

A PWI is one option for college. Sometimes PWIs are referred to interchangeably as historically White institutions (HWIs) to reflect their European founding and majority White population across time, even if they have started experiencing more diversity in recent years. Nearly all American colleges and universities fall into the PWI (or HWI) category. Although they number in the thousands and are distinct in many ways, some broad commonalities unite them.

The first broad commonality is that PWIs are no longer exclusively for Whites only as a matter of policy. Discrimination of any sort is forbidden by law. Many PWIs have made progress over recent years with respect to increasing raw numbers of non-White students. This is called *compositional diversification.* It is a necessary step toward full inclusion because students first have to be represented proportionally in order to be included culturally. Thus, to be clear, the doors of PWIs are open to all qualified students, regardless of race or ethnicity, in order to comply with the law.

The next broad commonality tempers the progress marked in the first. Although today's PWIs are not exclusively for White students by law, many minorities such as Blacks continue to be and feel excluded. Although PWIs have admitted non-White students under legal compulsion for decades, and some PWIs have made remarkable strides toward compositional diversification in recent years, Black students often are severely underrepresented on campus. It is not uncommon for a Black student to enroll in a course and have no Black classmates, especially in a STEM course. Even less common is a Black faculty member or senior administrator at a PWI who can serve as a same-race role model. Many academic departments at PWIs lack a single Black faculty member at all, and most senior level administrators at PWIs are White (and male).

Beyond the numbers, a deeper source of exclusion persists. Because many PWIs have a long history of racial segregation and/or discrimination against Blacks, marginalization and oppression can continue in unofficial ways even today. Despite the alleged progressive bent of individual college professors, the evolution of American higher education has largely followed the trajectory of broader American society. As unappealing as this sounds, the United States has been slow to include non-Whites fully. Efforts to diversify often focus on compositional diversification because it is measurable, but efforts fall short of full inclusion, which is far more challenging to assess and requires systemic change.

Defenders of the status quo at PWIs might demand proof of this exclusion beyond students' feelings and stories. Research suggests that exclusion comes in various forms at PWIs, and much of it is difficult to isolate because it is embedded so deeply in the fabric of the institution. Typically, racial exclusion can be observed in the traditions, curricula, and practices of these schools, which tend to place or privilege Europe and its aesthetics, values, and ideologies over all others. Whether intentional or not, this "Eurocentricity" often ignores, excludes, and devalues educational approaches of non-White cultures. Asian, Latin American, Middle Eastern, Native American, and African ways of living and learning are usually treated as topics of study or majors in the curriculum, if they receive any attention at all. Non-White students often struggle to see themselves reflected in the curriculum. In short, to attend a PWI usually means being educated explicitly or implicitly according to a cultural worldview that places Europe at the center and all other cultures as foreign or "other."

These factors at PWIs—that is, the Eurocentric ethos and primarily White racial population—are known to produce many race-based barriers for Black students. These barriers are added to the challenges faced by all students, producing a specific type of stress called *acculturative stress*. Acculturative stress occurs when Black students struggle to adapt to the foreign, largely Eurocentric, culture of a PWI. The result can be "an insufficient sense of belonging at the institution [which] stifles engagement and diminishes one's inclination to persist toward baccalaureate degree attainment" (Harper, 2009, p. 700). Even if a Black student at a PWI does persist to successful graduation, one study suggests only 29 percent feel their chosen college prepared them for life after degree completion (Gallup, Inc., 2015).

This does not mean all PWIs should be avoided. Despite their systemic challenges, our goal is not to discourage all Black students from pursuing a STEM degree at a PWI. Although the commentary provided in the preceding paragraphs may give that appearance, our goal is to provide an honest discussion of challenges so students are aware of them from the first year. However, we also devote significant space in the remainder of this book to highlighting strong STEM programs at PWIs that provide viable options for prospective Black STEM students.

In fact, today most Black students do choose a PWI, and some PWIs are doing notable work with Black STEM students. One example is Saint Mary's University of Minnesota, which was featured in an article by *Forbes*. Located in the city of Winona, this small Catholic college is renowned for its work with minority STEM students. Although minorities comprised just 10 percent of its class in 2008, roughly 35 percent of those 10 percent earned their degree in a STEM field. Campus leaders attribute this to their intentional effort across the institution to create a supportive, welcoming environment for all students. Another example is the all-women's Bryn Mawr College, in which 16 percent of Black undergraduate students graduated with a STEM degree between 2011 and 2014 (Cassidy, 2015). This is greater than the overall percentage of Blacks in the United States, and it shows that some PWIs can effectively support students of all races.

Still, these examples are rare, not the norm. Prospective Black STEM students entering their first year at a PWI are advised that they will probably face many systemic race-based challenges. Success is more likely when unknowns are decreased through awareness. Surprises can engender discouragement, high amounts of acculturative stress, and dropping out, particularly when a student endures several negative experiences leading to the conclusion that he or she does not belong. No one wants to feel like an outsider, much less in the already challenging environment of higher education. Awareness of potential issues prior to matriculation can lessen this sense of isolation. Likewise, awareness of resources available to help students navigate challenges can help. We will discuss several such resources later in this chapter.

Historically Black Colleges and Universities (HBCUs)

Even as more Black students consider a PWI for their STEM education, they should understand that other options exist. One example is a historically Black college or university (HBCU), which is a type of minority serving institution (MSI). For several years running, the top producer of Black engineers has been North Carolina A&T State University, which is an HBCU. In fact, HBCUs are responsible for some 40 percent of all Black engineers in the United States (The Network Journal, n.d.). Likewise, Xavier University of Louisiana in New Orleans is widely reputed to be the top producer of Black students who continue to medical school than any other college or university nationwide, including Ivy League schools such as Harvard and Yale (University Herald, 2012). Yet, contrary to many PWIs, which are often elevated on a pedestal and revered, HBCUs are often misunderstood and belittled. Therefore, we should explain what makes them distinct and relevant as choices for today's students, beginning with a definition.

According to the Higher Education Act of 1965, as amended, an HBCU is "any historically Black college or university that was established prior to 1964, whose principal mission was, and is, the education of Black Americans." An institution also must be accredited or making reasonable progress toward accreditation. Nearly 90 four-year, public and private HBCUs are in operation today. The total number of HBCUs, which includes two-year HBCUs, is approximately 107 as of this writing (U.S. Department of Education, n.d.). Students looking for a quality STEM education might consider an HBCU rather than a PWI.

In contrast to the dominant Eurocentric educational approach of most PWIs, the educational approach of HBCUs tends to be non-Eurocentric or even Afrocentric. We should clarify the following from the outset: The non-Eurocentric or Afrocentric nature of HBCUs does not mean HBCUs discriminate against non-Black students or that non-Black students are unable to receive an outstanding education at an HBCU. To the contrary, evidence suggests HBCUs deliver positive curricular and extracurricular experiences to Whites, Asian Americans, Native Americans, and Latinos (see Aregano, 2015; Arroyo, Kidd, Burns, Cruz, & Lawrence-Lamb, 2015; Arroyo, Palmer, & Maramba, 2015). As a category of institutions, unlike PWIs, HBCUs have never discriminated against any applicant on racial grounds. The non-Eurocentric or Afrocentric approach of many HBCUs simply creates a *different* learning environment than PWIs. In the spirit of choice, these schools offer students another option.

To illustrate the special HBCU-based educational approach for Black college student success, Arroyo and Gasman (2014) created a visual model based on decades of empirical research about the work of HBCUs. Although individual HBCUs vary in their strengths and weaknesses, the model generally depicts the tendency of HBCUs collectively to offer a different experience compared to PWIs. A brief overview of the HBCU-based educational approach follows.

The model begins with *relative accessibility*, which means HBCUs tend to accept highly prepared students along with those students who are underprepared or underserved due to their prior educational and socioeconomic settings. HBCUs are renowned for serving students who may not have been admitted elsewhere and transforming them into capable workers ready for a competitive marketplace upon graduation.

Key to their ability to accomplish this is a *supportive environment*. Once admitted, students benefit from a culture of support where faculty, staff, and administrators view student success and well-being as a personal mission. HBCUs are widely regarded as being more supportive of Black students than are PWIs.

During a student's progression through college, the HBCU-based approach blends three focuses: *achievement*, *identity formation*, and *values formation*. As expected, the institution works to promote the achievement of students through a quality education. Many casual observers fail to realize that HBCU students perform equal to, or better than, their non-HBCU counterparts. Although they comprise roughly 3 percent of all institutions of higher education in the United States, they produce 20 percent of Black degree-earners and a disproportionate number of Black STEM graduates (Palmer & Wood, 2012; Perna et al., 2009).

Figure 4.1   An HBCU-Based Approach for Black College Student Success

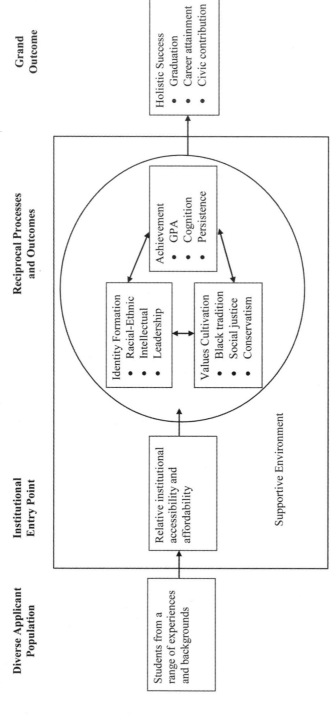

However, it is the addition of the two other elements in the model—identity formation and values cultivation—that truly distinguishes HBCUs. We might refer to the interplay of these elements as the HBCU "hidden curriculum." Black students at HBCUs benefit from environments that build strong identities across at least three dimensions: racial, leadership, and intellectual. In other words, they grow in confidence and understanding regarding their history and ability as Black Americans to perform at the highest levels. They also receive grounding in traditional Black American values such as an emphasis on their role in the community and working for social justice. Overall, the approach at HBCUs is interdependent and communal in nature. Although individual achievement is encouraged and prized, a sense of connectedness to a greater whole in a cooperative atmosphere—which is a non-Eurocentric or Afrocentric hallmark—is foundational to the HBCU process.

The final outcome of the HBCU-based approach is *holistic success*. In the same Gallup (2015) poll cited previously, 55 percent of Black HBCU graduates felt prepared for life after graduation compared to 29 percent of Black PWI graduates. This points to a significant difference between the types of education many Black students report receiving depending on the institution they choose.

Ultimately, college choice is a very personal decision. To repeat an earlier point, our goal is not to direct Black students toward or away from PWIs or HBCUs. The best college is the one that is best for the individual student. Students should pay attention to whether the institution "fits" their expectations and needs, and they should avoid selecting a school based on perceived reputation. Fit is especially important because both the first year of college and the STEM curricula will bring challenges regardless of institution. Proximity to home, cost (including tuition and scholarships), availability and quality of the desired program, and a host of other factors should be weighed carefully. The point underscored in this action step is that another salient factor might be whether the school is a PWI or HBCU. Students who have chosen the right institution will have reduced one major challenge, leaving them free to focus on others that might arise.

Table 4.1 summarizes several key factors Black STEM students should consider when choosing an institution.

ACTION STEP TWO: FOLLOWING KEY STUDENT-LEVEL STRATEGIES, PRACTICES, AND SKILLS

Whatever the challenges a Black STEM student is facing, regardless of institution, students should understand that no barrier is insurmountable. All barriers can be conquered. Students and institutions can do much to improve the chances that students will persist (or be retained) despite obstacles they might face. On an institutional level, colleges and universities—PWIs and HBCUs alike—have created many strategies and systems to support students. We will describe examples of institutional supports later in this chapter. First, we will discuss student-level strategies, practices, and skills that students can develop on their own. Putting these into practice as early as possible, even during one's senior year of high school and

Table 4.1   Factors to Consider When Choosing an Institution

Choosing the right institution is vital for a rewarding first year in college.
Transferring to another institution is expensive in time, energy, and money.
PWIs offer excellent opportunities, but may contain race-based barriers for Black STEM students.
HBCUs are an outstanding option for Black STEM students due to their special educational approach.

---

certainly over the summer, should give the student an edge when challenging times come.

Students can persist and succeed in the face of challenges by taking personal action. As Kuh, Kinzie, Schuh, and Whitt (2011) have observed, "What students *do* during college counts more in terms of what they learn and whether they will persist in college than who they are or even where they go to college" (p. 7). Although we suggested earlier that choosing the right college is a critical first action step, we agree with these authors as well: no hostile college environment is any match for a focused student who applies the right behaviors. Consistently executing research-based strategies, practices, and skills will improve students' chances of reaching the end of their college STEM journey with the required degree or degrees for a rewarding career in their chosen field. Taking self-directed action will also enhance productivity and enrich their overall experience. The purpose of this section is to discuss how to do so.

As added motivation for putting these tips into practice, much of what we cover in the following pages is applicable beyond school. Success in career and life requires a similar mind-set and approach as success in college. Students who develop a comprehensive personal success plan that works for them in college can be assured that their efforts will not be wasted in the "real world" because they are investing in their own future. We outline several of the most relevant strategies, practices, and skills for college success here, beginning with the need to prepare for opposition, or pressure, coming from peers.

Prepare for Opposition from Black Peers

As previously noted, Black STEM students are engaged in important work that will advance their own lives and the societal trajectory of their race. Despite the praiseworthiness of the commitment being a STEM major deserves, their peers are not always supportive. This includes, sometimes surprisingly, Black peers. Fellow Black students can be quite disparaging, owing in part to lack of shared values or misguided perceptions regarding the relationship between success and racial identity.

Researchers have found that Black peers and even some family members might criticize a highly motivated Black student for "acting White" (see also Chapter One) (see Fordham & Ogbu, 1986; Lundy, 2003; Thompson, Lightfoot, Castillo, & Hurst, 2010). The underlying notion is that academic success and being Black are at odds. In addition, among Black males, dedication to higher education might be perceived as incongruent with manhood or masculinity. This disconnect could result in a phenomenon called "cool pose," which "causes Black men to distance themselves from activities associated with White and feminine values, such as education" (Wood & Palmer, 2015, p. 4; see also Harris, Palmer, & Struve, 2011). When added to the typical peer pressures associated with being a serious college student (e.g., coercion to attend parties, engage in illicit or illegal behaviors, procrastinate, etc.), these racialized peer pressures might further discourage Black students from performing at their best.

Black students should be aware of these threats to success before entering their first year of college; however, awareness alone is an insufficient strategy. Locating and befriending like-minded peers before the semester begins or soon after classes start can create insulation from peer-to-peer negativity. Joining a learning community (LC), living-learning community (LLC), or other institutional support system, which we discuss later in the institutional supports section of this book, can facilitate these connections. Clubs, student organizations, fraternities and sororities, Black male initiatives (BMIs), Summer Bridge Programs, and community and religious groups can also provide sources for positive relationships. Studying and modeling the behaviors of high-achieving Black students can also provide both inspiration and concrete ideas for application. In recent years, more scholars have documented the mind-sets and habits of high-achieving Black students (e.g., Harper, 2012; Wood & Harris, 2013). Insights from their research appear throughout this section as well.

Anticipate Interpersonal and Institutional Racism

As indicated in the discussion of PWIs, preparation for racial challenges is another important first-year success strategy. Black students who enter college expecting a world without racism could end up demoralized and dropping out. Students who prepare ahead of time for a variety of hidden and direct racialized encounters will not be caught off guard. This is especially the case in PWIs and in STEM fields where Blacks are severely underrepresented and where their competency and right to enter those spaces might be challenged daily.

The recommendation to anticipate interpersonal and institutional racism in college simply acknowledges a reality that many people already know: College campuses are microcosms of everyday life. Even as racism is present in society, so it is present in college. Even today, reports of racial aggression on college campuses appear in local and national headlines (e.g., Almasy, 2015; Supiano, 2015; Wines, 2015). Failure to acknowledge this difficult reality is deceptive.

Equally as distressing as overt racism is the presence of hidden racism on college campuses. Hidden racism goes largely undocumented in the popular press but nevertheless carries potential negative consequences for those who live through it without a strategy for handling it. We can list many examples of hidden racism. Sometimes it manifests in the classroom when faculty members assume their Black students are academically inferior. This can feed the insecurities of Black students and lead to self-fulfilling negative prophecies.

Another example occurs when students or faculty insinuate that a Black student was "given" an undeserved spot in a school or program due to race. Misguided understandings of affirmative action and race-conscious admissions practices are often invoked. Charges might be levied that the Black student stole the rightful place of a more qualified White candidate. White resentment and hostility is expressed in these instances, with potentially negative impacts on the Black student's experience.

Among the most dangerous types of hidden racism are racial micro-aggressions resulting from White color-blind ideologies. Williams and Land (2006) explain that color-blind ideologies occur when "Whites systematically internalize racist attitudes, stereotypes, jokes, folklore, assumptions, fears, resentments, discourses, images, and fictitious racial scripts handed down through an elite discourse that fit into a dominant White post-civil rights world view of color-blind racism and anti-Black rhetoric" (p. 580). These beliefs and practices are particularly dangerous and difficult to challenge because many Whites who carry them are the same Whites who insist they are not racist. These ideologies can be so deeply engrained into the fabric of an institution and its stakeholders (students, faculty, administrators) that they might harm Black students' sense of belonging and performance subconsciously as they erode Black students' security and confidence slowly over time.

Due to the presence of racism in all its shades, scholars have argued "institutions must continue to improve the campus milieu so that Black students feel comfortable and supported to help facilitate their growth and development" (Wood & Palmer, 2015, p. 9). Yet this is difficult to achieve. Despite institutional efforts to counter racism and to become spaces of equality and diversity, colleges and universities often fall short of higher standards needed to change the milieu: equity and inclusivity.

The difference between the two ideas is important to understand. Many schools, especially PWIs, have created offices, departments, and directors in charge of increasing the numbers of non-White students and planning programming for them. These efforts are grounded in the well-intentioned but misguided idea that ending racism is a function of quantity. It is hoped that merely changing the racial composition of the student body will lead to a racial panacea. In reality, these surface efforts often leave the deeper aspects of the institution undisturbed and unaltered. Eurocentric curricula, severe underrepresentation of Blacks and other minorities in the faculty and administrative ranks, and the generally chilly racial climate of many college campuses must be disrupted so they can change.

College students—including those in their first year—can be active in the face of racism. Today, more and more Black students are participating in the democratic process to challenge inequities, stereotypes, and color-blind ideologies on their college campuses. Black students, together with other minorities and White allies, are taking a stand against policies, procedures, institutional cultures, and individuals who seek to perpetuate racism. Rather than waiting for an outsider or authority figure to change their surrounding environments, these students are exercising collective freedom and agency to lead the change they envision. While each student's chosen form of engagement should be a personal matter of conscience with the counsel of trusted advisors (e.g., family, clergy or other spiritual leaders, mentors), students should enter their first semester of college with the understanding that their involvement or lack thereof could be pivotal in the creation of a healthy, inclusive campus culture where they can thrive socially and academically. Participation in the democratic process is the right of all students. Indeed, if it were not for the actions of brave Black students crossing color lines in the 19th and 20th centuries, it is likely that PWIs would remain fully segregated now. Books such as this would not be considered, let alone written.

Prioritize Personal Mental Health

The next success strategy for surviving and thriving in the first year of college is to prioritize personal mental health. On college campuses nationwide, mental health of all types is emerging as one of the more urgent areas in need of attention. For the purposes of this book, we define mental health as a broad area that includes everything from situational stress, which includes the acculturative stress mentioned earlier, to diagnosed mental disorders. At best, poor mental health can lead to general malaise and underperformance (i.e., late work, failed exams, etc.). At worst, it can lead to self-injury and suicide.

Situational stress, which is most common among STEM college students, "is produced when one perceives the demands of a situation to exceed one's available resources" (Greer & Chwalisz, 2007, p. 388). Situational stress associated with school can result from rigorous schoolwork, maladjustment from being away from home, school-life balance, family, romantic relationships, friendship challenges, temporary or prolonged illness, or trauma to oneself or a loved one. Situational stress comes and goes as the environment changes or as a person learns to navigate the environment better.

On the other hand, mental disorders are more persistent and challenging in most cases. Examples of diagnoses include manic-depressive disorder (bipolar disorder), schizophrenia, obsessive-compulsive disorder, and clinical depression, to name a few. Although certain situations may make these disorders temporarily worse (or better), they are different from situational stress. Therapy and/or medication in the care of a trained psychologist, licensed clinical social worker (LCSW), or psychiatrist are often required. These professionals typically draw diagnoses from the *Diagnostic and Statistical Manual of Mental Disorders, Fifth Edition (DSM-5)*. Any situational stress or mental disorder can be complicated and compounded by substance abuse and poor habits related to diet, exercise, and sleep.

With respect to the Black community, mental health has received inadequate attention historically. Black students might experience additional race-related stressors compared to Whites—such as acculturative stress—especially when attending PWIs (Greer & Chwalisz, 2007). Among Black male students at PWIs and HBCUs, reasons for rejecting mental health care include negative stigmas, embarrassment, feelings of weakness, and cultural mistrust. Black female college students cite many of the same concerns as Black males, "possibly making them vulnerable to experiencing academic difficulties or dropping out" (Bradley & Sanders, 2003, p. 188).

Because of this, scholars are challenging colleges and universities to address mental health preparedness for Black students. Recommendations include establishing counseling centers and facilitating proactive programming and dialogue to remove stigmas. However, individual students should not wait for an institution to reach out before addressing their own mental health. Personal initiative is required. At the first indication of a problem, students should reach out to their institution's counseling center. Alternatively, students can seek community-based resources. This is a viable option if a college campus either lacks the appropriate personnel or the student feels uncomfortable with the environment for any reason. Most essential is that the student obtains assistance because time is of the essence where mental health is concerned.

Draw from a Faith Tradition

Faith, spirituality, and religion are deeply personal topics. Not all students share the same tradition, and some subscribe to no tradition at all. The purpose of this recommendation is not to prescribe a faith tradition or impinge on a student's right to practice any faith or no faith. However, we include it because research suggests faith holds value for Black college students of various traditions (see Mutakabbir & Nuriddin, 2016; Watson, 2006). Among those for whom faith does hold importance, including it in a holistic first-year survival strategy makes sense.

Black STEM students in particular might find significant grounding in their faith tradition. Jett (2013) documents this in his qualitative study of four Black male graduate mathematics and mathematics education majors. Each also earned his undergraduate degree in mathematics. Through interviews, "it became readily apparent that these men possessed convergent spiritual perspectives concerning their academic (mathematics) success" (p. 325). The researcher's study also incorporated his own experiences, which further demonstrated a connection between faith and STEM success. Importantly, this small-scale study comports with larger studies examining the relationship between faith-based practices and Black college student success (e.g., Mattis, 2000).

Key spiritual practices might be particularly helpful in a STEM student's daily and weekly routines. Meditation, prayer, scripture reading, and/or fellowship with fellow worshippers can provide an anchor and source of strength. In addition, Black STEM students can "be exposed to the literature and historical portraits of academically successful, spiritual African Americans" (Jett, 2013, p. 331). If these examples are not readily available through one's college or faith community, the student can locate examples in biographies and autobiographies on his or her own.

Gaining inspiration from successful STEM professionals who have maintained a strong spiritual core can help first-year students foster a sense of their own integrated purpose.

Maintain and Build Ties with Home

In higher education research, one of the ongoing debates related to minority students is the role of family in the student success journey. Specifically, the question is whether they should break away from their ties at home to form a new life at their college or whether they should maintain home ties. Some theorists (e.g., Tinto, 1993) have maintained that a clean separation from a student's home is essential. The idea behind this theory is that making this break will connect them more deeply to the institution, which is vital to retention and persistence toward degree completion. However, the practice of divorcing oneself from home to begin a new life in college might require going against one's subculture in harmful ways. The action of going out on one's own is built on Eurocentric principles such as individualism and autonomy that may be inconsistent with other subcultures (e.g., Black, Latino). As such, minority students whose values vary from the dominant majority culture might do better to deepen family ties than to weaken or sever them.

Especially for Black students at PWIs where the environment might be chilly or even hostile toward students of color, family can be an indispensable resource for surviving and thriving. Herndon and Hirt (2004) list several contributions that Black students' families make to their success: ongoing encouragement and support (e.g., financial, moral, spiritual, and social), socialization into issues and challenges pertaining to race in American culture, motivation, expectation-setting, and others. For these reasons, Black STEM college students who come from a strong family or community should recognize this asset and draw from it as needed.

Of course, not all home relationships are so positive and encouraging. Sometimes they are the source of stress. A student might become distracted trying to deal with issues at home, supporting family members, and/or feeling guilty for appearing selfish that they are advancing their own life while leaving others behind (even if that is not their motivation). If these pressures build up too much, the student might take an untimely leave of absence or drop out of college completely.

The lesson for the Black STEM student is to draw support from home when it is available and advantageous. Distancing oneself from home during the first year of college can close a student off to one of their greatest assets. All the same, a point may come where a degree of separation becomes necessary, especially when individuals in the home community are behaving in a distracting manner and creating doubt in the student's mind about whether degree completion is a justifiable goal. Degree completion greatly increases one's chances of securing a personally profitable and meaningful career that will benefit one's family in tangible and intangible ways. Therefore, except in rare cases where a student truly must leave school to tend to family business, staying in school and finishing on time is a better long-term decision for both individuals and their current and future families.

Connect Early and Often with Professors

All strategies presented in this book are important for success-oriented STEM students. However, one of the *most* important strategies is to connect early and often with professors. We will offer practical tips for interacting with professors, but first we should examine what the research says about the importance and benefits of faculty-student connections.

Faculty-student interactions deliver many specific benefits that contribute to success. A national survey found that the "three most potent elements linked to long-term success for college graduates" were "1) they had at least one professor who made them excited about learning; 2) the professors cared about them as people; and 3) they had a mentor who encouraged them to pursue their goals and dreams" (Gallup, 2015, p. 15). Kezar and Maxey (2014) reviewed relevant literature on this subject and identified three overall benefits of faculty-student interaction: increased student aspirations; improved interest, passion, and motivation for learning; and enhanced academic self-confidence. Further, the researchers noted that students of color and first-generation students derive the most benefits from engagement with faculty.

These findings agree with Hinderlie and Kenny (2002), who found that student-faculty relationships are particularly critical for Black undergraduate students. The researchers conducted a study of 186 full-time, traditional-age Black college students at six private, academically competitive PWIs. They concluded that, "when all sources of support are considered simultaneously, support from instructors is significantly associated with academic adjustment" (p. 337).

Black STEM students should understand that the availability and quality of faculty support could be very different between institutions. Not all colleges are the same in terms of faculty support. One might be attracted to a large school with a national reputation without realizing that many classes are taught by graduate students, and faculty are relatively disengaged from the classroom because they are pursuing their own research and writing. Across PWIs, the challenge can be locating faculty who provide the type of support Black students need to thrive.

Conversely, HBCUs tend to excel in the area of faculty support (Flowers, Scott, Riley, & Palmer, 2015). When Fries-Britt and Turner (2002) interviewed Black students about their experiences at an HBCU, they found that "A part of what makes the HBCU feel like home is the individual attention that students receive from faculty and staff" (p. 320). The researchers continued by saying, "Black students who attend HBCUs perceive teachers and administrators as going out of their way to assist them and individually meet their needs" (p. 320). Faculty members at HBCUs are often seen as "going far beyond the call of duty to provide encouragement and support" (p. 321). One way they do this is by mentoring students in their care, which is significant for long-term success postgraduation.

Wherever they choose to attend, first-year students should be proactive. Forming relationships with faculty members early and visiting them often is one way to do this. Even the most supportive instructors often serve many students in addition to fulfilling other duties associated with their employment (e.g., preparation for class, research projects, serving on university committees and other working groups). While taking care not to monopolize a faculty member's time, students should intentionally seek out their faculty members early in the semester follow this up with frequent contact throughout the semester. When possible, face-to-face communication is preferable to communication at a distance. Visits during office hours are one of the best ways to connect. E-mails and phone calls are less desirable because they lack the personal feel of in-person conversation. If the instructor allows self-selected seating in the classroom, students should choose a row near the front. Prominent physical location can promote engagement during class. It reduces the risk of distraction and sends a subtle message to the instructor that the student is serious about learning.

Finally, the student should realize there is such a thing as coming to a professor "too late," especially when the student is struggling or behind on work. Going to see a professor for the first time a few weeks before the semester concludes—or even waiting for the midterm—could leave the instructor's hands tied. Students should contact their instructors at the first sign of a problem to allow ample time for proactive solutions.

Savvy first-year students realize that the choices they make early in their college careers—even when it comes to interacting with faculty in introductory or general education courses—will have ramifications later. A poor freshman GPA could hinder graduate school plans, whereas a strong freshman GPA will create positive momentum. Patterns of engaging faculty members ingrained early could impact how a student connects with faculty as an upperclassman, which in turn could impact the quality of letters of recommendation for graduate school or jobs. Faculty members might not write letters of recommendation for students who they do not know or who have submitted subpar or late work. Therefore, from the first day of the first week of the freshman semester, success-oriented students will waste no time connecting with faculty.

Collaborate with Faculty Members

Connecting with faculty members is the initial step to a successful first-year experience in college. However, eager students need not stop there; they can seek collaborative relationships as well. Collaboration involves working together to produce original research for presentation and publication. At least four benefits come from student-faculty collaboration. First, students receive deeper mentoring than they would by only connecting in structured settings (e.g., office hours, classrooms). Second, students gain valuable technical skills due to participation in advanced work. Third, students begin building their own research profile. Fourth, students may become part of informal and formal networks of emerging and established scholars. Keeping these benefits in mind can motivate a student to pursue collaborations.

Although a collaboration of real magnitude is highly unlikely during the first year, students can begin learning about the research interests of their eventual professors and seeking opportunities to interact with those professors about their work. The surest way to achieve some measure of collaboration is by signing up to participate in an undergraduate research symposium or science-based club. Many college campuses hold a symposium annually for their own students and offer numerous clubs. Undergraduate research journals also exist, so eager students might find an opportunity to make a contribution under the mentorship of a professor. Expressing a desire to participate, and then following through with an excellent presentation, project, or paper, can help a student build a reputation as someone a faculty member might work with at advanced levels later.

To reiterate, full collaborations during freshman year are exceedingly rare. Yet students should not expect to be noticed unless they take measures to become noticeable. Despite the fact that faculty usually seek graduate students or advanced undergraduate upperclassmen for their personal research teams, exceptional first-year students can begin distinguishing themselves from the crowd with the right mind-set and follow through from the earliest weeks of the fall semester.

Build Noncognitive Variables

Although scientific and other forms of cognitive skills are vital to STEM success, noncognitive variables are also undeniable factors in determining how a student fares in college. Noncognitive variables can include skills, abilities, or other factors or inputs such as positive self-concept, realistic self-appraisal, successfully handling the system, preference for long-term goals, availability of a strong support system, leadership experience, community involvement, and knowledge acquired in a field. Another key variable for Black males has been identified as "grit" (i.e., persistence, determination, and motivation). Successful first-year students will focus on building their whole self with attention to these and other non-cognitive factors, in addition to traditional cognitive training and development.

Implement a Time Management System

The final recommendation is among the most practical but applicable to all students: implement a time management system. Time management is life management. A finely crafted system of time management will benefit a student throughout life. Habits formed while young provide a critical foundation for the future. Real-world careers in fast-paced, complex environments can involve similar challenges as college with overlapping deadlines and multiple stakeholders (i.e., customers, coworkers, supervisors, etc.).

Securing financing; planning a course schedule; registering for courses; obtaining required course materials; locating quality, affordable housing; making friends; and dealing with peer pressure can be daunting. Add to these overlapping and conflicting deadlines, and students can quickly fall behind if they are not actively managing their workload. Professors provide syllabi, which contain readings and assignments with due dates for their individual courses. Although the syllabi are helpful for navigating each course, they are often not coordinated between courses. Except in rare cases, professors do not communicate with each other in the planning of their semesters; instead, they plan the assignments by their own schedule without regard to what might be taking place in other courses. This is the system at most colleges, so change is unlikely. Students must adapt through personal time management techniques.

At the core of an effective strategy is maintaining a planner. As soon as the semester's assignments and due dates are provided, the information should be transferred to a planner. While this is an important first step, it is not time management. Recording due dates for assignments tells a student only three things: when the assignment is due, whether the due date closely coincides with work due in other courses, and whether the due date conflicts with personal events such as a birthday. Thus, entering due dates in a planner is a poor time management strategy simply because it fails to address the real questions of when the student should begin working on the assignment and how the student should structure the work and at what intervals. To manage one's time for success, a student must invest a significant amount of effort in creating a *plan of work* for each assignment in each course. To illustrate the complexity of this process, imagine a five-course load, with five assignments per course. This translates into 25 individual due dates over the course of a 16-week semester, which means 25 interwoven plans of work that are at various stages of starting and stopping at all times. (Note: Many courses have more than five assignments.)

After a comprehensive, semester-long plan of work has been developed, then the even more challenging part begins: managing the plan as the semester unfolds. Students set themselves up for failure when they believe that life will pause during a semester. It does not. Illness, a family emergency or a death, or any number of situational stressors could arise during a semester. The practical implication is the need to revisit the remaining work plan and make midcourse changes. Many professors will not accept late work, regardless of the excuse. If they do accept it, the work might come with a point penalty. Even if points are not deducted, deeper learning is stunted because late assignments are often rushed. Although many students claim to work best "under pressure," this is counter to how good work actually happens: slowly, deliberately, methodically, and with many revisions. A properly executed plan of work will place a student ahead in many cases; therefore, the variety of issues that are sure to arise during a semester will not result in academic failure.

In this section, we have covered behaviors students can implement that, if practiced consistently, will empower them to succeed in virtually any environment. Whether or not students can change their environment, they can always choose their response to it. Next, we focus on added-value support systems that are available at many colleges and universities. These support systems, in combination with choosing the right institution and practicing personal success strategies, can all but ensure a positive freshman year.

**Table 4.2   Key Student-Level Strategies,
Practices, and Skills for First-Year Success**

Prepare for opposition from Black peers.
Anticipate interpersonal and institutional racism.
Prioritize personal mental health.
Draw from a faith tradition.
Maintain and build ties with home.
Connect early and often with professors.
Collaborate with faculty members.
Build noncognitive abilities.
Implement a time management system.

Table 4.2 details the key student-level strategies, practices, and skills for first-year success as we have defined them in this chapter.

ACTION STEP THREE: TAKING ADVANTAGE OF INSTITUTIONAL SUPPORT SYSTEMS

Although students must develop strategies and skills for their own college success in pursuit of a STEM career, today's colleges and universities offer many support systems to complement students' efforts. Rather than blaming struggling students as the sole cause of their failures—as though they possess a natural deficit of motivation or ability—more institutions are taking some responsibility. Particularly in the case of first-year students, institutions are realizing the payoffs of investing resources in their success. Theoretical research underscores the importance of institutional responsibility in the student success equation, especially for Black American students and other students of color. Additionally, empirical studies have suggested that institutional investments in such support systems yield positive returns in first-year retention rates.

Before giving examples of institutional support programs at a variety of colleges and universities, it is important to note that institutional support systems generally fall into certain broad categories or types. Not every form of support is appropriate for all students. Savvy students will understand both the types of supports available as well as their own availability and needs in order to create the most advantageous match. The types of institutional supports we cover here are student support centers, living-learning communities (LLCs) and learning communities (LCs), and multi-institution partnerships.

First, many institutions have dedicated *student support centers*. University employees operate these centers with funding from the school, donors, or grants. Typically, student support centers are housed in a location convenient to students with extended availability before and after business hours. Services provided can range from content tutoring to skills development to registration in some cases.

Faculty might refer struggling students to the support center at their institution. At institutions where midterm grades are issued, staff at these centers might receive a list of struggling students to conduct proactive outreach. Examples of student support centers will be provided in the coming pages.

Another type of institutional support is known as a *living-learning community* (LLC) or *learning community* (LC). These are classified in the higher education literature as high-impact practices (HIPs). Research demonstrates connections between these programs and student success (see Brower & Inkelas, 2010; Tinto, 2012). As the name implies, LLCs are primarily residential in nature, while LCs tend to be more open to residential and commuter students. Some colleges create these communities for students in specific majors or STEM students in general. Others are developed around a multidisciplinary or interdisciplinary theme that has some relevance for STEM majors. Students might take a course together while also participating in cocurricular or extracurricular activities designed to enhance the learning experience by allowing students to interact with each other and with professors in nontraditional and informal ways, thereby increasing the sense of community. The curriculum also becomes more interesting because what is learned in the classroom is given application through activities.

As an aside, it is worth noting that not all LCs are created equal. Arroyo, Ericksen, Walker, and Aregano (2016) have suggested that HBCUs have the potential to offer more appealing and impactful LCs for Black students in part by respecting and drawing from their community cultural wealth and alternative capital, combined with the special HBCU-based approach for Black college student success. Nonetheless, the basic LC model, which enhances students' interaction with each other, tends to be valuable for a broad variety of students, including and especially Black STEM students.

Another available support is the *multi-institution partnership*. As with the other two support systems mentioned previously, we will provide illustrations of key partnerships later in this chapter. Often, these partnerships come about because institutions find that they can benefit greater numbers of students when they pool resources. Partnerships can be regional or national, can be connected to grant funding or institutional funding, and can include resource sharing, transfer agreements, or another form of program.

Finally, it is worth repeating that some types of colleges and universities are more naturally supportive of Black and other minority students, regardless of the range of additional support services they offer. Writing about MSIs, which includes HBCUs, Conrad and Gasman (2015) noted that in 2011, MSIs "enrolled about one-quarter of all undergraduate students in the United States and a disproportionate percentage of students of color" (p. 10). More importantly, these schools are reputed to have "an institution-wide commitment to treating every student as an individual" (p. 273) and a commitment to their entire curriculum to make it more relevant to students' experiences and communities. The authors explained further, "Students come to college for degrees that lead to jobs. They also come to college as agents in their own right, as people who are seeking to find their own places in their worlds.

They need colleges that provide them with opportunities to study the stories of their cultures and their places in them and also to reflect on the ways in which their futures are emerging from their pasts" (p. 273). For STEM students, this can help them maintain interest and see the relevance of what they are studying to real-world problems they are being trained to solve.

In all, whether attending an MSI such as an HBCU, or whether attending a PWI, a Black STEM student should be encouraged. Resources of many types are available with their support in mind. In the following page, we give examples of specific support programs at a variety of institutions. These are only some illustrations of what is taking place at many schools nationwide. The selected examples hint at the wide variety of available support programs. Additionally, these examples demonstrate the breadth of subject areas that fall under the STEM acronym. We should point out, of course, that these examples are current at the time of this writing. Name changes, funding sources, and organizational realignment might result in these specific programs no longer being offered in the future or being offered in different ways. Readers should contact their institutions directly to learn what they offer and how to become involved.

Also important to note is the varied requirements for entry and goals of the programs. Some are intended to serve academically underprepared students. Others are competitive and designed to attract high-achieving students. When investigating available programs, students should pay close attention to any entry requirements. Alignment between the student and the program is critical for gaining all intended benefits.

The Center for Women in Technology (CWIT)

Web site: http://www.cwit.umbc.edu/about/
Location: University of Maryland, Baltimore County (UMBC), Baltimore, MD
Population served: Focus on women, but open to men also;
includes a focus on racial/ethnic diversity

The Center for Women in Technology was formed at the University of Maryland, Baltimore County, a PWI, with the recognition that women are generally underrepresented in STEM fields. This includes women of underrepresented minorities. According to the Web site, the program's goals include sustaining and strengthening a vital scholar program for undergraduates committed to increasing the representation of women in Information Technology and Engineering (ITE) fields; fostering a supportive community for all women in ITE at UMBC; improving gender climate in the College of Engineering and Information Technology; and broadening the pipeline of talented women interested in ITE with K–12 outreach programs. Practical initiatives include peer mentoring, women in technology workshop series, industry mentoring, and an LLC. The program also contains the Parents for Women in Technology group, which facilitates parental engagement in support of students in the program.

Howard University Science, Engineering, and Mathematics Program (HUSEM)

Web site: http://www.howard.edu/sem/husem.htm
Location: Howard University, Washington, D.C.
Population served: Focus on underrepresented minorities

Designed to increase the numbers of underrepresented minorities attaining STEM degrees, the Howard University Science, Engineering, and Mathematics Program is housed in Howard University, which is known as one of the most elite Black colleges. The program is grant funded by the National Science Foundation (NSF) and National Semiconductor Research Corporation Education Alliance (NSRCEA). The initiative's three major objectives are to form a seamless high school to PhD STEM pipeline, to improve retention of current STEM students, and to produce capable leaders for the engineering and scientific community. Accordingly, five major programs are part of HUSEM, per its Web site: Funded Undergraduate Research Experiences; weekly and group tutoring sessions; personal, professional, and academic mentoring; Distinguished Scholars Fellowship program; and early intervention for students who are prone to drop out of STEM courses. Of note, this is one of many STEM support programs available at Howard University.

Minority Engineering Program (MEP)

Web site: https://www.udayton.edu/engineering/diversity/minority_engineering.php
Location: University of Dayton, Dayton, OH
Population served: Focus on underrepresented minorities

The Minority Engineering Program is an initiative of the University of Dayton, a PWI, for African American, Hispanic American, or Native American STEM students. According to the Web site, activities include a summer residential program; academic success workshops; professional development workshops; collaboration (tutoring and mentoring) with fellow students; registration in the same math, chemistry, and physics courses with a cohort (they call this "clustering"); and individual advising with the program director. Additionally, all members of this program receive a $3,000 annual scholarship and qualify for additional scholarships and internships through their minority leaders program. The University of Dayton also offers a weeklong summer bridge program for incoming minority STEM students. Funding for this program comes from the school and the Virginia W. Kettering Foundation.

STEM House

Web site: http://www.ncat.edu/student-affairs/housing/
communities/llc/stem.html
Location: North Carolina A&T State University, Greensboro, NC
Population served: All students

STEM House is an LLC located at North Carolina A&T State University, a well-known HBCU. Participants must apply to be part of this LLC, which is located in a campus residence hall. All participants are STEM majors. According to the Web site, "Residents participate in a variety of academic, personal development and career exploration activities intended to build a sense of community and increase understanding of STEM disciplines." A variety of activities and experiences are offered to this group throughout the year. Students are referred to as "scholars" to reflect the following additional requirements: members are first-year freshmen majoring in biology, environmental sciences, chemistry, engineering, physics, technology, or mathematics; have an interest in research and a desire to pursue a PhD; and have a minimum 3.0 GPA and 900 SAT score.

North Carolina A&T also offers the Technology and Innovation LLC. This is a separate group from STEM House that is open to all first-year technology majors. Special emphasis is placed on exploring technology's global societal impact.

Academic Excellence (ACE) Program

Web site: http://ace.ucsc.edu
Location: University of California Santa Cruz, Santa Cruz, CA
Population served: Focus on underrepresented minorities

The Academic Excellence (ACE) Program's stated goal is to provide academic support and increase diversity among the University of California, Santa Cruz, STEM majors. An innovative program located in a PWI, the purpose of ACE is to bring together motivated STEM students in supplemental study sessions designed to complement what can be impersonal lectures due to their size. According to the Web site, "We bring STEM students together in active learning problem solving sessions that supplement several large math and science lectures. We help you understand the lecture and textbook through concept specific worksheets that you and your classmates work on as a team." Using a model that states students should study 15 hours per week outside lectures, ACE ensures that one third of that time is "guided and focused." In the process, participants also learn valuable skills such as teamwork and time management.

Dozoretz National Institute for Mathematics and Applied Sciences (DNIMAS)

Web site: https://www.nsu.edu/cset/dnimas/
Location: Norfolk State University, Norfolk, VA
Population served: All students with emphasis on African Americans

Located at the historically Black Norfolk State University, since 1985, DNI-MAS has been addressing "the severe shortage of minority scientists" through a comprehensive four-year program. Students apply in the fall from high school for admission into the program the following fall. All DNIMAS students receive a full, four-year scholarship from Norfolk State University. Additionally, DNIMAS scholars receive "a three week, pre-matriculation summer session, intensive science curricula, reserved microcomputer labs for student use, research internships, field trips, projects, career counseling, and seminars." DNIMAS also functions as an LLC to enhance the experience further. Prospective applicants are encouraged to contact the program director through the Web site for more details on the competitive application process.

Purdue University Minority Engineering Program (MEP)

Web site: http://www.purdue.edu/mep/
Location: Purdue University, West Lafayette, IN
Population served: Focus on underrepresented minorities

Originating at Purdue University in 1974, a PWI, the Minority Engineering Program's mission is "to advance engineering learning, discovery, and engagement in fulfillment of the Land Grant promise through outreach, recruitment, and retention of historically underrepresented students in their pursuit to become extraordinary Purdue engineers." This takes place through a variety of programs, including precollege programs, campus visitation, freshman transitional boot camps, freshman orientation seminars, mentoring, academic support, scholarships, and other forms of outreach. High school students or their supporters can complete an information request form on the program Web site, and prospective and current students can visit the program's office located on campus.

North Carolina State University Minority Engineering Programs (MEP)

Web site: https://www.engr.ncsu.edu/mep/
Location: North Carolina State University, Raleigh, NC
Population served: Focus on underrepresented minorities

North Carolina State University, a PWI, created the Minority Engineering Program to support the recruitment and retention of racially underrepresented students interested in becoming engineers or computer scientists. Along with offering the traditional array of supports, one of this program's unique features is the Overnight Recruitment Stay. According to the Web site, this "weekend is geared towards admitted minority engineering students who are interested in learning more about our campus and the rigors of completing an engineering degree. The Overnight Recruitment Stay will allow students to see first-hand what life as a minority engineering student entails and gain insight into the opportunities available for a successful undergraduate career at NC State University." Registration is required, and details are sent to all admitted minority students in February.

Vanderbilt Summer Science Academy

Web site: https://medschool.vanderbilt.edu/vssa/vanderbilt-minority-
summer-research-program
Location: Vanderbilt University, Nashville, TN
Population served: Members of federally recognized groups who
are underrepresented in the sciences

The Vanderbilt Summer Science Academy at Vanderbilt University, a PWI, offers qualified students a special summer experience: a paid summer research internship in the laboratory of an outstanding Vanderbilt scientist. Housing is also provided. According to the Web site, the program "provides an opportunity for undergraduates to experience first-hand the research that is advancing our understanding of both normal biology and human disease, and the opportunity to develop new therapies and cures to the illnesses that face our society." Formal mentoring throughout the summer is complemented by a research project and organized activities, culminating in a formal presentation at the end of the summer. Research projects can focus on any of the following areas: cardiology and cardiovascular disease, biochemistry, biological sciences, cancer biology, cell and developmental biology, cellular and molecular biology, human genetics, microbiology and immunology, molecular physiology and biophysics, neurosciences, and pharmacology. This is a selective program that requires an application with letters of recommendation.

University of California Irvine Minority Science Programs (MSPs)

Web site: http://port.bio.uci.edu/about/
Location: University of California Irvine, CA
Population served: Underrepresented minorities

The Minority Science Programs at University of California, Irvine, are designed to increase the number of underrepresented minorities in biomedical research careers. The programs are funded in part by a National Institutes of Health (NIH) grant. According to the Web site, "MSP participants benefit from early exposure, continuous research training and faculty mentoring." Initiatives include paid research internships, access to the latest computer technology, tutoring, academic advising, scientific writing, and participation in national conferences. The program also has cultivated a network of partners "to facilitate the transition from high school through community college, baccalaureate and master's degrees to PhD careers in biomedical research."

As noted earlier, the institutional support programs mentioned here demonstrate the wide variety of initiatives existing nationwide with the goal of guiding

Black students toward STEM careers. Next, we turn to examples of partnership programs with the same purpose. These involve multiple institutions working together rather than one institution working on its own. Students attending schools that have active partnerships can feel confident in the commitment of that school for their success, as well as in the existence of resources to match. When comparing partnerships and institution-specific programs, we should note that neither is necessarily better than the other. Students should always evaluate and match their needs to available programs, and seek the programs that represent the best fit. Some typical examples of multi-institution partnership are as follows.

Pacific Northwest Louis Stokes Alliance for Minority Participation (PNW LSAMP)

Web site: http://depts.washington.edu/lsamp/
Lead institution: University of Washington, Seattle, WA
Population served: Underrepresented minorities

This alliance includes five institutions in the three-state Pacific Northwest Region of Washington, Idaho, and Oregon. In addition to traditional support initiatives such as tutoring, student members have access to the following benefits: paid internships, paid research, funding for conference travel, priority for study abroad, STEM textbook checkout, industry tours, and opportunities to serve as a mentor and ambassador to current and prospective students. According to the Web site, a main focus of the initiative is "providing workshops and services to ensure that 95% of the LSAMP-affiliated students are exposed to information about graduate school preparation."

Greater Philadelphia Region Louis Stokes Alliance for Minority Participation (GPR LSAMP)

Web site: http://www.philadelphiaamp.org
Lead institution: Drexel University, Philadelphia, PA
Population served: Underrepresented minorities

Similar to its Pacific Northwest Regional counterpart just discussed and other Louis Stokes Alliances across the nation, the Greater Philadelphia Region Alliance includes multiple institutions combining HBCUs and PWIs. They include two- and four-year schools with research and nonresearch emphases. Specifically, nine are included in this partnership: Cheyney University, Community College of Philadelphia, Delaware State University, University of Delaware, Drexel University, Lincoln University, New Jersey Institute of Technology, University of Pennsylvania, and Temple University. Significantly, this alliance has existed since 1994, indicating its strength borne of success. STEM students attending any of these institutions should contact their department for more information on current initiatives.

Extreme Science Internships (ESI)

Web site: http://www.morgan.edu/school_of_computer_mathematical_and
_natural_sciences/internships_and_fellowships/extreme_science_internships.html
Lead institution: Morgan State University, Baltimore, MD
Population served: Underrepresented minorities

In partnership with the Hopkins Extreme Materials Institute located at Johns Hopkins University, Morgan State University runs this internship program for selected undergraduates. Students receive funding for 8–15 week internships at a research university or laboratory (e.g., Army Research Laboratory) on a project related to extreme dynamic environments. Participants will benefit from connections with practicing scientists and engineers, in addition to gaining knowledge and skills. This program requires an application.

Blandy Experimental Farm Research Experiences for Undergraduates Program (REU)

Web site: https://sites.google.com/site/blandyreu/
Lead institution: University of Virginia, Charlottesville, VA
Population served: All students

The Blandy Experimental Farm Research Experiences for Undergraduates Program is a partnership among the University of Virginia; Howard University; Rowan University; Universidad de Puerto Rico, Bayamón; and Universidad de Puerto Rico, Mayagüez. According to the Web site, this partnership "provides research fellowships to students interested in ecology and environmental science." The primary goal of the program is "to teach students to formulate testable hypotheses about important ecological and evolutionary questions." This includes developing skills in experimental design, data collection, analysis, and critical reading of primary scientific literature. Students are also taught how to prepare, compile, and communicate their results in a way that will be understood by scientists and the public. Awards, which are competitive and require an application, include stipends, along with a meal budget, free housing, and a supplies and research-related travel budget.

Center for Science of Information (CSoI)

Web site: http://www.pathwaystoscience.org/programhub.aspx?sort=STC
-Purdue-CSoL
Lead institution: Purdue University, West Lafayette, IN
Population served: Underrepresented minorities

Along with Purdue University, eight other institutions have partnered to create the Center for Science of Information: Bryn Mawr College; Howard University;

Massachusetts Institute of Technology; Princeton University; Stanford University; University of California, Berkeley; University of California, San Diego; and University of Illinois at Urbana-Champaign. This program seeks to promote the following academic disciplines: bioengineering, bioinformatics and genomics, biomedical engineering, biotechnology, computational sciences, computer and electrical engineering, computer sciences, general math, psychology and behavioral sciences, and telecommunications. According to the Web site, the program "aims to broaden the Science of Information community by providing a pathway or 'channel' towards a wide range of opportunities for undergraduates . . . who are members of underrepresented groups." Entry into this competitive program is by application. Participants receive mentoring from an active researcher or scientist on a project during the fall and spring semesters, as well as a financial stipend, while attending classes.

Table 4.3   Examples of Institutional Support Systems for STEM Students

Programs	Objectives
The Center for Women in Technology	The Center for Women in Technology was formed at the University of Maryland Baltimore County, a PWI, with the recognition that women are generally underrepresented in STEM fields. This includes women of underrepresented minorities. According to the Web site, the program's goals include sustaining and strengthening a vital scholar program for undergraduates committed to increasing the representation of women in Information Technology and Engineering fields; fostering a supportive community for all women in Information Technology and Engineering at UMBC; improving gender climate in the College of Engineering and Information Technology; and broadening the pipeline of talented women interested in Information Technology and Engineering with K–12 outreach programs. Practical initiatives include peer mentoring, women in technology workshop series, industry mentoring, and an LLC. The program also contains the Parents for Women in Technology group that facilitates parental engagement in support of students in the program.
Howard University Science, Engineering, and Mathematics Program (HUSEM)	Designed to increase the numbers of underrepresented minorities attaining STEM degrees, the Howard University Science, Engineering, and Mathematics Program is housed in Howard University, which is known as one of the most elite Black colleges. The program is grant funded by the National Science Foundation (NSF) and National Semiconductor Research Corporation Education Alliance (NSRCEA). The initiative's three major objectives are to form a seamless high school to PhD STEM pipeline, to improve retention of current STEM students, and to produce capable leaders for the engineering and scientific

(*continued*)

Table 4.3   (*Continued*)

Programs	Objectives
	community. Accordingly, five major programs are part of HUSEM, per its Web site: Funded Undergraduate Research Experiences; weekly and group tutoring sessions; personal, professional, and academic mentoring; Distinguished Scholars Fellowship program; and early intervention for students who are prone to drop out of STEM courses. Of note, this is one of many STEM support programs available at Howard University.
Minority Engineering Program	The Minority Engineering Program is an initiative of the University of Dayton, a PWI, for African American, Hispanic American, or Native American STEM students. According to the Web site, activities include a summer residential program; academic success workshops; professional development workshops; collaboration (tutoring and mentoring) with fellow students; registration in the same math, chemistry, and physics courses with a cohort (they call this "clustering"); and individual advising with the program director. Additionally, all members of this program receive a $3,000 annual scholarship and qualify for additional scholarships and internships through their minority leaders program. The University of Dayton also offers a weeklong summer bridge program for incoming minority STEM students.
STEM House	STEM House is an LLC located at North Carolina A&T State University, a well-known HBCU. Participants must apply to be part of this LLC, which is located in a campus residence hall. All participants are STEM majors.
Academic Excellence Program	The Academic Excellence (ACE) Program's stated goal is to provide academic support and increase diversity among the University of California, Santa Cruz, STEM majors. In the process, participants also learn valuable skills such as teamwork and time management.
Dozoretz National Institute for Mathematics and Applied Sciences (DNIMAS)	Located at the historically Black Norfolk State University, since 1985, DNIMAS has been addressing "the severe shortage of minority scientists" through a comprehensive four-year program. Students apply in the fall from high school for admission into the program the following fall. All DNIMAS students receive a full, four-year scholarship from Norfolk State University. Additionally, DNIMAS scholars receive "a three week, pre-matriculation summer session, intensive science curricula, reserved microcomputer labs for student use, research internships, field trips, projects, career counseling, and seminars." DNIMAS also functions as an LLC to enhance the experience further. Prospective applicants are encouraged to contact the program director through the Web site for more details on the competitive application process.

(*continued*)

Table 4.3   (*Continued*)

Programs	Objectives
Purdue University Minority Engineering Program	Originating at Purdue University in 1974, a PWI, the Minority Engineering Program's mission is "to advance engineering learning, discovery, and engagement in fulfillment of the Land Grant promise through outreach, recruitment, and retention of historically underrepresented students in their pursuit to become extraordinary Purdue engineers." This takes place through a variety of programs, including precollege programs, campus visitation, freshman transitional boot camps, freshman orientation seminars, mentoring, academic support, scholarships, and other forms of outreach.
North Carolina State University Minority Engineering Program	Along with offering the traditional array of supports, one of this program's unique features is the Overnight Recruitment Stay. According to the Web site, this "weekend is geared towards admitted minority engineering students who are interested in learning more about our campus and the rigors of completing an engineering degree. The Overnight Recruitment Stay will allow students to see first-hand what life as a minority engineering student entails and gain insight into the opportunities available for a successful undergraduate career at NC State University."
University of California Irvine Minority Science Program	The Minority Science Programs at University of California, Irvine, are designed to increase the number of underrepresented minorities in biomedical research careers. The programs are funded in part by a National Institutes of Health (NIH) grant. According to the Web site, "MSP participants benefit from early exposure, continuous research training and faculty mentoring." Initiatives include paid research internships, access to the latest computer technology, tutoring, academic advising, scientific writing, and participation in national conferences. The program also has cultivated a network of partners "to facilitate the transition from high school through community college, baccalaureate and master's degrees to PhD careers in biomedical research."
Pacific Northwest Louis Stokes Alliance for Minority Participation	This alliance includes five institutions in the three-state Pacific Northwest Region of Washington, Idaho, and Oregon. In addition to traditional support initiatives such as tutoring, student members have access to the following benefits: paid internships, paid research, funding for conference travel, priority for study abroad, STEM textbook checkout, industry tours, and opportunities to serve as a mentor and ambassador to current and prospective students. According to the Web site, a main focus of the initiative is "providing workshops and services to ensure that 95% of the LSAMP-affiliated students are exposed to information about graduate school preparation."

(continued)

Table 4.3 (*Continued*)

Programs	Objectives
Greater Philadelphia Region Louis Stokes Alliance for Minority Participation	The Greater Philadelphia Region Alliance includes multiple institutions combining HBCUs and PWIs. They include two- and four-year schools with research and nonresearch emphases. Specifically, nine are included in this partnership: Cheyney University, Community College of Philadelphia, Delaware State University, University of Delaware, Drexel University, Lincoln University, New Jersey Institute of Technology, University of Pennsylvania, and Temple University. Significantly, this alliance has existed since 1994, indicating its strength borne of success.
Extreme Science Internships	In partnership with the Hopkins Extreme Materials Institute located at Johns Hopkins University, Morgan State University runs this internship program for selected undergraduates. Students receive funding for 8–15 week internships at a research university or laboratory (e.g., Army Research Laboratory) on a project related to extreme dynamic environments. Participants will benefit from connections with practicing scientists and engineers, in addition to gaining knowledge and skills. This program requires an application.
Blandy Experimental Farm Research Experiences for Undergraduates Program	The Blandy Experimental Farm Research Experiences for Undergraduates Program is a partnership among the University of Virginia; Howard University; Rowan University; Universidad de Puerto Rico, Bayamón; and Universidad de Puerto Rico, Mayagüez. According to the Web site, this partnership "provides research fellowships to students interested in ecology and environmental science." The primary goal of the program is "to teach students to formulate testable hypotheses about important ecological and evolutionary questions." This includes developing skills in experimental design, data collection, analysis, and critical reading of primary scientific literature. Students are also taught how to prepare, compile, and communicate their results in a way that will be understood by scientists and the public. Awards, which are competitive and require an application, include stipends, along with a meal budget, free housing, and a supplies and research-related travel budget.
Center for Science of Information	Along with Purdue University, eight other institutions have partnered to create the Center for Science of Information: Bryn Mawr College; Howard University; Massachusetts Institute of Technology; Princeton University; Stanford University; University of California, Berkeley; University of California, San

(*continued*)

Table 4.3   (*Continued*)

Programs	Objectives
	Diego; and University of Illinois at Urbana-Champaign. This program seeks to promote the following academic disciplines: bioengineering, bioinformatics and genomics, biomedical engineering, biotechnology, computational sciences, computer and electrical engineering, computer sciences, general math, psychology and behavioral sciences, and telecommunications. According to the Web site, the program "aims to broaden the Science of Information community by providing a pathway or 'channel' towards a wide range of opportunities for undergraduates . . . who are members of underrepresented groups." Entry into this competitive program is by application. Participants receive mentoring from an active researcher or scientist on a project during the fall and spring semesters, as well as a financial stipend, while attending classes.

CONCLUDING THOUGHTS

This chapter has provided critical advice for surviving and thriving in a student's first year of college. Success does not happen overnight, nor does it occur by accident. Intentional actions such as choosing the right type of institution, preparing oneself to navigate race-based barriers and other challenges common to Black students in their first year, and taking full advantage of available institutional resources are some of the ways the best students can set themselves up for success. Because the first year of undergraduate school is the most pivotal year for many students, giving it extra attention is both appropriate and wise.

In the next chapter, *Choosing a STEM Major*, we offer students an inside look at the process of transitioning to a STEM degree program. The process is more involved than picking a major and taking classes. We describe concepts and practices related to progression, personal responsibility, advising, online and on-campus programs, and seeking multidisciplinary and interdisciplinary preparation.

CHAPTER FIVE

Choosing a STEM Major

In Chapter Four, we discussed ways to survive and thrive during the first year of college. We learned that the freshman year is one of not only excitement and possibilities but also special challenges that can lead to students dropping out before their sophomore year. If met proactively, students can succeed amid the challenges. Students should take at least three action steps: choose the right institution; follow key student-level strategies, practices, and skills; and take advantage of institutional support systems. First-year STEM students are encouraged to return to these action steps often as part of a comprehensive success plan.

The current chapter discusses the process of choosing or declaring a STEM major. Some colleges and universities require students to declare a major as early as their first semester or during the freshman year, but they do not provide much assistance with making the choice. Others engage students in a prescribed period of exploration that lasts through the freshman year. Regardless of an institution's system for making this declaration, some advice applies to all students.

On the surface, choosing a major may seem as simple as matching a student's broad area of interest with a particular academic discipline and then earning passing grades in the required courses. Students who envision becoming a biologist choose to major in biology, students who are interested in a career in computers choose to major in computer science, and so forth for chemistry, physics, mathematics, psychology, and others. However, for STEM students, the reality is far more complex than pointing and choosing based on a Web site or course catalog. This chapter attempts to demonstrate the complexity of choosing a major while also providing practical advice for making the process manageable.

We begin the chapter with a concept called *progression*, which addresses moving toward on-time graduation on a predictable time line. No matter the major a student chooses, attention to on-time graduation is vital to success. Next, we discuss the value and benefits of academic advising. However, we also suggest that students must own the advising process. They must recognize that the final responsibility for scheduling the right courses, succeeding in those courses, and determining a career path is theirs. After advising, we focus on course delivery. Growing numbers of courses and programs are offered via traditional on-campus formats, as well as online. Students should be aware of potential opportunities and drawbacks associated with each course delivery approach.

Finally, we close the chapter with a special interdisciplinary challenge for Black STEM majors to integrate the social sciences and humanities in their degree program. Emphasizing social science and humanities preparation in addition to technical education is vital for producing graduates who will enter the workplace prepared to be leaders; understand the broader, deeper implications or consequences of their work; know how to work with diverse people and knowledge bases; and engage the world as productive citizens. This ought to be the goal of "higher" education, that is, not only to receive a set of skills but also to experience holistic formation. If the preceding foundations are in place, declaring a major will be smoother and should lead to fewer regrets or changes once the major is declared.

PROGRESSION: ALWAYS KEEPING THE END IN MIND

We begin with the notion of progression, which requires always keeping the end in mind. Few students, if any, begin college with the intention of leaving without a degree. First-year students enrolling in a four-year college or university do so with the goal of completing within four years so they can begin a rewarding, lucrative STEM career or enter graduate school. Yet, as Azziz (2015) notes in "How to Graduate on Time" for the American Council on Education, the American tradition of categorizing undergraduate institutions as two-year and four-year is "alarmingly inaccurate." In fact, 530 of the more than 580 public four-year colleges and universities in the United States fail to graduate their full-time students in four years—or what is known as on time. In other words, for myriad reasons, most students in so-called four-year programs take longer than five, six, or more years to complete them.

As demonstrated in Chapter Four, Black college students can encounter a variety of barriers that hinder or stop progress. However, despite the dropout factors already addressed in this book, one factor has not been addressed: a basic lack of progression from freshman to sophomore to junior to senior status on a standard, predictable four-year time line. This lack of progression might be due to taking the wrong courses, switching majors, or not registering for enough credit hours per semester. We address all of these issues throughout this chapter, beginning with the last: not registering for enough credit hours per semester.

Success-oriented undergraduate STEM majors should ensure they are completing classes at the rate of five per semester. Unfortunately, many college students do not practice this principle, which might be due, in part, to the fact that the U.S. government defines "full time" as 12 or more credit hours for financial aid purposes.

Students can be registered for what is technically full time, but they might actually be off track for on-time graduation from their very first semester in college without realizing it before the damage has been done. Time is a college student's most valuable limited resource, but after it is spent, it is impossible to reclaim.

This problem has led national organizations such as Complete College America to create "Full-Time is Fifteen" and "15 to Finish" slogans (Complete College America, 2014) in an effort to remind students what is required to graduate on time. Although a student might take fewer than five courses during a given semester while still qualifying for federal financial aid and later make up the missing hours through summer school or by taking an overload of 18 or 21 hours, this approach is not advisable. Students attending school during fall and spring semesters with the goal of graduating within four years should be aware that on-time graduation is mathematically impossible unless they are taking a full 15 credit hours each fall and spring. Overall, a STEM student should never take any action regarding course load or registration without first asking the question: How will this impact my anticipated graduation date?

ACADEMIC ADVISING: WHAT IT IS AND WHO IS RESPONSIBLE

The progression issue outlined previously dovetails with our next topic, academic advising. Whose job is it to ensure that a student is well-informed about requirements for on-time graduation, as well as all other critical information for success? We will see shortly that advisors are important to those goals. However, one party is most essential: the student.

Before discussing the role of university advisors, we should be clear that students bear the ongoing and final responsibility for choosing courses, selecting a major, and keeping track of their progress. Although this may be an unsettling thought for young and inexperienced college students, it is important to underscore this point first. Advising offered through an institution is no substitute for students' full engagement in planning—and staying on top of—their academic journey. No professional advisor removes the final burden of responsibility from an individual student. In the end, the student will have to retake a failed course or fill missing gaps in their degree program—not the advisor. Students must *own* their degree, beginning with mastering the degree-seeking process.

One way to master the degree-seeking process is by applying the concept of studying. Many students mistakenly believe that studying refers only to class assignments and examinations. In truth, a student should study the course catalog first. This means reading the catalog, beginning at the first page, and mastering its contents. Students should understand all college-wide, departmental, and programmatic policies and procedures, as well as the general education curriculum and the curriculum for their desired major. There is no substitute for studying the catalog in detail.

Based on this information, students should map their progression plan rather than waiting for someone to do it for them. This progression plan should list the courses required for on-time graduation, when they are offered, and the best way to group them in each semester. If classes are filled or sections are unavailable, the plan should also contain alternates. The plan need not be perfect, but it should represent the student's best effort at making sense of the system. Students who do this place themselves in a position for success. They will know to ask their advisor the right questions, respectfully challenge potentially wrong information, and ultimately safeguard against incompetent advising that could delay graduation.

If this task sounds challenging, it is. However, the task is not as challenging as balancing five classes per semester or earning a rigorous STEM degree while navigating "real life," nor is it as challenging as retaking failed or missed courses and experiencing delayed graduation for months or years as a result. Every extra month a student spends in school is lost potential income in a new STEM career. That reason alone should be motivation for a student's initiative. Moreover, just as no one should trust their finances, auto repairs, or physical health to an industry expert without educating themselves, neither should a college student rely solely or even mainly on an advisor who could make a mistake.

Only after completing this due diligence planning should a student go to see an advisor. Depending on a student's level of experience, the plan he or she puts together may be imperfect and require adjusting. First-generation students or students without friends or family who can help guide them may wish they had a mentor to aid them. As we will show in this chapter, advisors can fill this mentoring role. Nonetheless, because ultimately students are responsible for their progression and graduation, we recommend that they fully educate themselves on all policies and requirements rather than following any single advisor's word blindly.

Given everything we have stated about student responsibility, one might wonder why an advisor is necessary and what an advisor does. A good advisor is an important partner in the success of today's undergraduate student when used properly. Academic advising directly influences student development. According to Folsom, Yoder, and Joslin (2015), "Master advisors, deftly adapting approaches and strategies within a conversation, teach students to solve problems and make decisions, challenge them to think in new ways, and help them to articulate and create pathways to their educational goals" (p. 1). A good advisor serves a larger purpose than helping a student select courses. In fact, good academic advising is a form of teaching. Advisors can use their interactions with students, especially at points of distress, to help them reframe the situation so they have a sense of positive self-concept, control, and motivation.

He and Hutson (2016) have identified five approaches to advising. Students are encouraged to learn which approach their institution or individual advisor uses so they can engage their advisor appropriately. One model, *information-based* advising, is the most "hands-off" approach. The advisor's job is focused on sharing information with a student regarding the process, regulations, and policies of the institution. In a second advising model, *intervention-based* advising, advisors build relationships with students, assist them during preenrollment and preregistration, and track students to identify those who are at risk so they can intervene immediately. Third on the list of models is *holistic development*, which goes a step further to support students' academic, moral, and personal growth. Advisors seek to foster noncognitive skills in their advisees. Fourth, some institutions and advisors adopt the *student learning outcome* model. A major goal of this advanced model is to employ teaching and learning practices to help students reach independence. Finally, in the *strength and asset building* approach, advisors learn their students' strengths and then help students "to develop positive reconstruction of past experiences, recognize alternative ways to leverage their assets for success, and establish positive outlooks to become resilient in their future personal and professional lives" (He & Hutson, 2016, p. 219).

Regardless of the model an institution or advisor adopts, best practices in advising suggest at least five components should be in place for effective advising: the conceptual, the informational, the relational, the technological, and the personal. *Conceptually*, advisors should be aware of the latest education theory related to student development and learning. *Informationally*, advisors must possess intimate knowledge of an institution's laws, policies, procedures, and resources available to students. *Relationally*, advisors should know how to build rapport with students so they can enjoy positive, productive interactions. *Technologically*, advisors should be experts in navigating the advising software used at their institution. Finally, *personally*, advisors should have self-knowledge that provides them grounding and confidence as they interact with students through sometimes challenging situations. Advisors without personal grounding can experience self-doubt, which can hinder effective service to students. The best advisor will ground their practice in these five components, and a student should expect that they do.

Cultural competence is also an attribute of good advising. This function is especially critical for Black STEM students in a predominantly White institution (PWI) where they might be part of a very small cohort of non-White students. At PWIs, the type of "capital" (i.e., knowledge and culture) that Black and other racial minority students bring with them tends to be misunderstood and undervalued. Capital that is valued by majority populations tends to revolve around monetary wealth, social connections, and ability to enter and navigate the institutions of the dominant culture. However, as Strayhorn (2015) and Yosso (2005) point out, Black and other minority students often bring with them other forms of capital, typically rooted in collectivist or interdependent cultures, which can also be used to promote their success. Advisors should "see students as actors, agents of their own destiny in this cultural space. Students bring cultural wealth—not deficits—with them." Taking on the role of "cultural navigators," advisors *work together* with students "to dig deep into their cultural repertoires and identify the wealth they bring to campus and the ways to deploy it in this setting that may be decidedly new to them" (Strayhorn, 2015, p. 59).

Historically Black Colleges and Universities (HBCUs) and PWIs are likely to have advisors who are capable cultural navigators, either by training or because they share the student's culture. However, a student should not assume that an advisor is culturally aware or sensitive, no matter their race. In the event a student's advisor is culturally unaware or insensitive, and if a student cannot switch advisors, then the student should recognize this as another race-based barrier that must be overcome, similar to the challenges we covered in Chapter Four. Overall, the equation for success is a student prepared to meet every challenge on his or her way to successfully completing a STEM degree.

Finally, we should broach the concept of career exposure in relation to advising. To aid a student in making an informed choice when selecting a major, exposure to jobs they might enter is invaluable. Often this requires contacting professionals in a given field and asking to speak with them about what they do—or even visiting them on the job. This process is informal and is different from an internship or an introduction that a career services office might provide. For this informal process, an advisor might be able to play a role in assisting students with networking to make initial introductions and productive ongoing connections. Aspiring STEM students are encouraged to have this conversation with their advisors about reaching out to STEM professionals for informal dialogues, as it might aid greatly in evaluating options leading to the choice of a major.

COURSE DELIVERY: ON CAMPUS OR ONLINE

Another important topic in connection to declaring a major is course delivery. For centuries, most colleges have offered a one-size-fits-all approach to course delivery. Although there is historical evidence that some distance learning took place in European and American higher education during the 1700s and 1800s, this was rare. Most college students went to physical classrooms, surrounded by peers and a professor, on brick-and-mortar campuses. Students' primary concerns revolved around choosing the right courses, taught by preferred professors, and navigating to the assigned building and classroom as scheduled. Moreover, there is a rich history in U.S. higher education of students living on campus in residence halls, and studies have associated residing on campus with increased student persistence.

Off-campus study became more widespread in the late twentieth century. Falling under the umbrella of distance education, more colleges started offering low-tech correspondence courses. Students would receive a spate of course materials delivered through regular post (i.e., "snail mail"), and they would return completed assignments to professors in the same fashion. Eventually, technologies such as cassette tapes, VHSs, CDs, and fax machines aided in the speed of delivery and communication while enhancing the quality of presentation. Nontraditional students found correspondence courses particularly useful because their flexibility could accommodate the lives of working adults with families. Still, comparatively few students participated in these courses of study. Although some full degree programs emerged under this structure, STEM programs tended to require on-campus study due to their hands-on nature.

Major changes began rippling through the arena of distance education in the mid-1990s and early 2000s. The advent and popularization of personal e-mail and the World Wide Web allowed colleges to reduce lag time in communication even more while dramatically improving content and teaching approaches. Blackboard, Inc., which was founded in 1997, quickly became a trusted course delivery platform that is in use at many higher education institutions today. In fact, some 80 percent of top academic institutions and 92 percent of top academic degree programs currently use a Blackboard learning system (Blackboard, Inc., n.d.).

Because of these developments, today's college students have more options than ever. Potential STEM students can anticipate an opportunity to take at least some courses online, even if they are traditional on-campus students. Some colleges offer blended or hybrid classes, which split the course delivery between in-person and virtual formats. Online courses a student might take include general education core requirements such as a lower-level English, history, or psychology; an upper level elective; or possibly even a major STEM course. Some schools also offer an entire STEM major in the form of an online degree completion program. Degree completion programs require a student to have already taken their general education requirements, but they then allow the student to complete a degree fully at a distance.

Examples of institutions with robust online STEM offerings are Florida State University's online degree completion programs in computer science (BA or BS), and Old Dominion University's online degree completion programs in computer science, computer engineering technology, or information systems. Other institutions offering some form of online course or program delivery for STEM degrees include the following: Drexel University, Syracuse University, DePaul University, University of Maryland University College, and University of Florida, to name only some. This list is not at all comprehensive or representative but rather illustrates the variety of colleges taking online education seriously. Many institutions today have a department, school, or college of distance education or distance learning, which houses information on that institution's available courses and programs. Students are encouraged to investigate options for course and program delivery at the school in which they are enrolled.

As students conduct an investigation regarding what their school offers, they also should honestly evaluate their fit for online education. Too often, students sign up for a particular course—whether on campus or online—too hastily. In so doing, they fail to assess properly whether their learning style and personal habits are suited for an online course. Perhaps they sign up hastily because traditional on-campus courses are full, because they do not like a professor or the scheduled time of an on-campus course, or because they hope the online course will be more convenient (or easier). Later in the semester—often when it is too late—they realize a crucial truth: online courses are not for everyone.

The mere fact that online courses and programs exist does not mean all students will flourish in them. Colleges might begin an online program to serve an institutional vision as much as—or even more than—students. Rovai (2009) observed that an "increasing number of traditional universities are transforming themselves" to offer online education because they "seek to become global institutions" (p. xi). To reiterate, the goal of global reach in itself is not unethical, but it does not equate automatically to what is best for each student. Indeed, some institutions enter the online education arena because they want to grow their brand recognition, increase their enrollment, and improve cash flow. For-profit colleges in particular have come under fire in recent years for unethical practices and low graduation rates. Thus, considerations about what is best for an individual student may not be taken into account, and students should be aware of this potential disconnect.

Some scholars have examined and scrutinized the trend of online education at HBCUs specifically. HBCUs overall have been slower than PWIs to adopt online education as a means of program or course delivery. One reason could be that HBCUs fear losing the sense of tradition that comes from being on an HBCU campus. Another reason might be the lack of resources and infrastructure to support a robust online program. Additionally, some pedagogical experts (e.g., Gallien & Peterson, 2004; Rovai, Ponton, & Baker, 2008) argue that the preferred learning style of many Black students is best served in a high-touch, group-based, interdependent physical setting. The independent, autonomous learning environment of many online courses could pose undue challenges to such learners.

Although not discouraging institutions and students from entering online education, Arroyo (2014) offered a cautionary model of potential hidden costs that students and schools—especially HBCUs—should consider. The model is grounded in the notion that the distinctive HBCU-based educational approach is, indeed, a highly individualized model that delivers many intangible benefits to students (Arroyo & Gasman, 2014). An HBCU attempting to expand regionally, nationally, or globally through online learning should be aware of two laws associated with scaled-up education that might do unintended damage to HBCU distinctiveness: It requires a natural push toward standardization, and it tends to reduce human freedom and individuality. Although this does not happen in every online environment and does not mean HBCUs or Black students should avoid online education, these tendencies are a cautionary call for institutions and students to consider before rushing into the distance education arena.

Importantly, online education can be adapted to HBCU culture and to multiple learning styles of diverse students. Proper course design and the right instructor make a critical difference. Still, all students should investigate online education, understanding the potential challenges, rather than assuming the fit is right. While examining fit, some key questions a student can ask include the following:

- Do I have the right temperament for online college?
- How well do I function as an autonomous (self-starting) student?
- How high is my need for an in-person community of learners?
- What hardware and software will I need to access lessons and complete all assignments?
- Do I have the resources to purchase additional technology if I need it?
- What is my familiarity and proficiency with computers, e-mail, the Internet, online research, and so on?

- Am I romanticizing online education as an easier or more convenient way of earning a degree, or am I fully aware of its challenges?

When these questions are asked and fully answered, then a student can move forward confidently.

Regardless of on-campus or distance status, all STEM students should become active in their major department. College can be isolating. Participation in departmental student associations, clubs, research symposia, honors societies, study groups, and the like are ingredients to a rewarding experience as a STEM major. All traditional on-campus programs offer continuous opportunities for student engagement, and many online programs are demonstrating innovation in connecting students to the campus, department, and one another.

INTERDISCIPLINARY CHALLENGE

To conclude this chapter, we want to address the topic of interdisciplinarity and to issue an interdisciplinary challenge to all STEM majors. *Interdisciplinarity* is the "process of answering a question, solving a problem, or addressing a topic that is too broad or complex to be dealt with adequately by a single discipline or profession" (Klein & Newell, 1996, p. 3). As we will illustrate shortly, STEM professionals who have competency across multiple disciplines—and who can skillfully integrate those disciplines—will be in a better position to address the most critical problems facing individuals and societies today. Consequently, the interdisciplinary challenge is a call for all STEM students to integrate the social sciences and humanities into their course of study and to take risks in applying their broad knowledge innovatively so they might emerge from college well-rounded and fully competitive.

Of course, the road toward expert-level interdisciplinarity is long and requires intentional effort in knowledge-building and skill-building. Different disciplines tend to be grounded in their own empirical assumptions, use specific research methods, and, in general, encourage very different ways of thinking about a given issue. A tendency of STEM majors is to focus solely on the disciplinary content and skills necessary for their desired field, primarily because the thought of focusing on other disciplines might seem like a distraction at best, if not completely overwhelming. However, because true interdisciplinary understanding and skill takes many years to develop, it should begin at the undergraduate level or earlier. STEM students in their freshman through senior years can begin fostering their interdisciplinary capacity—or their "whole-brain" experience—in many informal and formal ways.

One means of becoming interdisciplinary is by developing and following a multidisciplinary course of study. A student can do this by compiling a reading list of core, seminal texts in the social sciences and humanities. Diverse fields such as political science, psychology, sociology, philosophy, religion, art, and literature should be included in this reading list. While progressing through their prescribed

STEM coursework, they can intentionally reserve a small block of time each day (e.g., 15 minutes) to read from one of these texts. Students can also attend workshops, special speaker events, or even conferences outside their major. This provides important exposure to other ways of looking at problems they might face as STEM professionals. More formally, students can add a social science or humanities minor to their degree program. Extra-ambitious students may want to double major. Over time, these informal and formal efforts will result in an impressive and priceless reservoir of knowledge that students can use to engage in interdisciplinary work.

Even while STEM students are developing basic multidisciplinary competency, they should begin engaging in interdisciplinary research. In recent years, interdisciplinary scholars (e.g., Repko, 2012; Repko, Newell, & Szostak, 2011) have produced research methods and guides designed specifically to facilitate integrative projects. Eager STEM students can draw from these texts when they participate in undergraduate research symposia to develop and present interdisciplinary projects through poster sessions, paper presentations, or other formats. To reiterate our earlier point, the expectation is that the most advanced interdisciplinary research requires many years to cultivate; therefore, students should begin attempting such projects with courage early in their college career. Effort invested at the novice level will accumulate and lead to intermediate and advanced abilities later.

We can list many examples of ways mature interdisciplinary STEM professionals can use their expertise. Scientists who are developing and testing a new drug on humans should be conversant in the field of ethics, realizing that just because science *can* perform a certain experiment, does not mean it *ought* to perform the experiment. Psychologists who study the brain as a physical organ can avoid reducing people to "machines" by grappling with the philosophical difference between the brain and mind, along with exploring the age-old mind-body connection. A botanist who is focused on environmental problems can filter her research and efforts through lenses of politics and economics to gain a better understanding of forces driving the problems, as well as potential holistic solutions. Computer scientists can learn about entrepreneurship so they can effectively bring their ideas to market. Cybersecurity professionals can gain fluency in another spoken language (e.g., Russian, Mandarin, Arabic, Spanish, etc.), as well as study other world cultures, which will broaden their job opportunities immensely. In addition, an orthopedic surgeon who is treating combat amputees might study psychological and religious notions of identity to understand how the loss of a limb might impact their patient beyond the physical. In turn, this understanding will aid them in partnering with these individuals to experience fullness in the midst of loss. These are only some examples, and they are very narrow. The real world ways in which interdisciplinary research and practice make a difference are too complex in type and number to describe in a single book. Students are encouraged to conduct interdisciplinary discussions with each other, with their professors, and with other professionals. They should also read case studies to gain exposure to the needs and possibilities.

Related to building broad disciplinary knowledge, STEM majors also might want to seek training in leadership, management, and team-building. This recommendation dovetails with some of the noncognitive abilities we suggested students build in Chapter Four. Rarely will a STEM professional work alone in isolation from others, and it is impossible for one individual to master all disciplines needed to address the world's most intractable dilemmas. STEM professionals are needed who can function productively in fast-paced, challenging environments in teams that are high-energy, serious-minded, and diverse.

Individuals are also needed who can rise to the top of the team as effective managers and leaders. For this, STEM students who study principles of management (e.g., Tulgan, 2007), leadership (e.g., Sinek, 2014), and teamwork (e.g., Lencioni, 2002) are needed. Due to the underrepresentation of Blacks in STEM fields, intensive and intentional self-preparation to fill the top roles in teams and organizations is perhaps even more necessary than for overrepresented groups. Attaining the top position in a White-dominated team or organization might be challenging for a racial minority, but it is necessary if society is to realize an equitable distribution of power and influence in coming generations.

In this chapter, we discussed key principles and actions for choosing a STEM major, which are summarized in Table 5.1.

CONCLUDING THOUGHTS

In this chapter we covered salient, foundational principles and actions associated with choosing a STEM major. Declaring a course of study is more involved than completing paperwork and registering for a prescribed set of courses. Undergraduates who apply the principles and take the actions suggested in this chapter will experience fewer setbacks and will profit immensely in their chosen STEM program.

The next chapter, *Continuing on to Graduate School in STEM*, focuses on the mind-sets and practical steps necessary for earning a master's or doctorate degree in a STEM discipline. Students should not wait until their junior or senior years of college to begin preparing for graduate studies. We describe why early, consistent preparation is important, as well as key ways students can prepare themselves for advanced study in their area of choice.

Table 5.1   Key Principles and Actions for Successfully Choosing a STEM Major

Progression: Always taking and passing at least 15 credit hours per semester

Academic Advising: Taking personal responsibility while partnering strategically with an advisor

Course Delivery: Fully investigating online and on-campus options

The Interdisciplinary Challenge: Seeking broad preparation for addressing complex problems

CHAPTER SIX

Continuing on to Graduate School in STEM

In Chapter Five, we discussed how choosing a STEM major is best viewed as an intricate, multifaceted process, not a one-time decision that is hastily made. Students should devote continuous attention to progressing through their college degree at a rate consistent with on-time graduation. Advisors play a vital role as guides, but students should take the time to study all policies, procedures, and requirements on their own. Students should also construct their own schedule for review and input by an advisor, rather than waiting on an advisor to do it for them. Although challenging, these actions ensure a student's full ownership of the degree-seeking process and provides a safeguard in the event of incompetent advising. We also explained that degree program-delivery options require scrutiny and that students should enroll in online courses and programs only after they have fully investigated their fit. Finally, STEM students should intentionally develop interdisciplinary competency, which begins with multidisciplinary study and includes experimenting with interdisciplinarity in their research projects. Real-world rewards await students who cultivate expertise beyond the narrow confines of their own discipline.

The current chapter discusses continuing on to graduate school in STEM. For the purpose of this chapter, we group master's and doctoral programs together under the heading of graduate school. In some cases, a student can proceed directly from a bachelor's degree to doctoral studies, bypassing a master's program. Alternatively, a student might enter a master's program first or complete a master's program without proceeding to a doctoral program. In all cases, graduate school represents a different environment compared to the undergraduate level, and it requires a different approach.

Graduate school is important for aspiring Black STEM professionals in today's competitive economy. Data suggest that some form of graduate training is often a prerequisite to operating at the highest levels of a STEM field and is associated with higher earnings and quality of life. However, Blacks and other minorities are highly underrepresented among graduate degree earners in the United States. Because of this underrepresentation, this chapter begins with advice about how STEM undergraduates can prepare for graduate school. The most competitive and advantageous graduate school opportunities tend to come to students who began amassing the appropriate experiences early, rather than waiting until their senior year of college. In addition, this chapter covers tips for navigating graduate school so students emerge successful. Many of these tips are also relevant for advanced undergraduates who are most serious about becoming influencers in their field.

The most successful students will draw wisdom and inspiration from a variety of sources. Therefore, in addition to this chapter, we encourage students to read other materials. One excellent resource is *Building on a Solid Foundation: A Guide to Graduate School for Students at Minority Serving Institutions* (published by the Penn Center for Minority Serving Institutions). Although the title indicates the guide is for students at minority serving institutions (MSIs), the content is appropriate for all undergraduate students who envision attending graduate school. A variety of additional resources are also available (e.g., Gaudet, 2015), which students can locate online, in magazines, or in books.

PREPARING FOR GRADUATE SCHOOL

With the importance of a graduate degree in STEM established, we can turn our attention to preparing for graduate school. First, preparation for graduate school should begin as early in a student's educational career as possible. Ideally, students lay the foundation during the K–12 years by ensuring they enter undergraduate school with strong personal discipline and academic fundamentals. Certainly, by the time an undergraduate STEM student declares a major, the preparation for graduate school should be well under way.

In some respects, preparation for graduate school looks similar to preparation for undergraduate college. Academics must be in order, and grade point average (GPA) matters. Students with average or poor GPAs could see their options for graduate school greatly diminished, if not eliminated all together. Research suggests that cumulative GPA is significantly related to graduate school enrollment, and many undergraduate students aspire to attend a graduate school only to stop short of applying and enrolling after realizing their grades fail to meet the minimum standards. This suggests a disconnect among some students between their hopes and dreams and actual abilities. Although a trend in graduate admissions is currently under way for a "holistic review" of candidates beyond GPA and test scores, many programs continue to have a minimum GPA requirement that winnows the field of applicants automatically. Therefore, we underscore again that GPA matters.

Consequently, undergraduates who want to go to graduate school may face some difficult decisions regarding balancing academics and social life. Dedication to graduate preparation is demonstrated by choosing to study, spending time in a laboratory, or working on a project rather than socializing with friends. Ideally, a student will form a circle of like-minded friends who share the same values and goals so the student can avoid isolation and loneliness in the academic journey. A cooperative community where the student receives and gives peer support around academics is worth seeking and building, especially for minority students who are accustomed to a community-based, interdependent approach to their life and work. This remains true even though, as we will see shortly, developing a high level of independence will be necessary in graduate school.

In addition to academics, a STEM student focused on graduate school should consider strategic participation in other preparatory activities. Presenting research projects in undergraduate research conferences or symposia provides invaluable experience, adds incredible value to a list of accomplishments, and increases a student's interest in STEM. More specifically, students participating in undergraduate research activities gain clarity regarding future career options, build stronger technical and communication skills, create a science identity, improve self-efficacy, and attend graduate STEM programs at higher rates.

Where possible, students should seek to work under one of their professors to assist with their research in either a formal situation (e.g., the college or department offers an undergraduate assistantship) or an informal situation (e.g., if no such opportunity is available or it is already taken). Students should be willing to engage in the most menial tasks, never getting ahead of themselves by believing they deserve a bigger role than they are assigned. A good professor will reward diligent work, and a student should recognize that the best way to learn is by investing sweat equity at the "bottom." In the end, the result is the same: students gain experience that tuition money cannot buy, along with long-lasting relationships to match.

Students should also engage in networking, and professors in a student's department are the first level of the network. Students should realize that their professors often have strong working relationships with professors at other schools, including graduate schools. These relationships can open doors through letters of recommendation and personal introductions to the right people. Other levels of a student's network are important as well. When attending symposia or conferences, a student should seek memorable interactions with persons of influence in their field. Realizing such persons are approached frequently *for* things, the most successful students will seek ways to form relationships of service *to* such persons so that they are remembered for their willingness and ability to add value rather than merely take.

The process of networking can lead to a small circle of strong relationships that result in being recruited to a graduate school via an unsolicited offer. Although rare, it is not unrealistic that a highly prepared student might secure multiple offers from programs that want the student to enroll due to the value he or she brings. The student would be given a research or teaching assistantship or fellowship, which covers the full tuition and pays a stipend for living expenses. The graduate assistant or fellow is matched with a scholar in the department, who mentors the student, collaborates with the student, and becomes the student's thesis or dissertation chair and eventual biggest champion when the time comes for a postdoc or employment reference. To reiterate, however, receiving multiple unsolicited offers from graduate schools offering a full assistantship or fellowship is not the norm.

More typical is that undergraduate students seeking to attend a graduate school engage in a standard choice process where they apply rather than being recruited. According to English and Umbach (2016), the undergraduate choice process has been studied extensively (e.g., Perna, 2006), but far less research on the graduate choice process exists. The researchers conceptualized that the typical graduate choice process follows a sequence of aspiration to attend graduate school, application to a graduate school, and enrollment in a graduate program. While in the aspirational phase, students should investigate what graduate programs are available, the requirements for admission, and where they are located. After conducting this preliminary search, students should engage in a deeper investigation to narrow the pool of institutions to which they will apply.

To aid in the process of selecting a school, the Institute for Broadening Participation (2014a) recommends the following action steps:

1) **Become familiar with the prospective department**. This means contacting the department, visiting the department, and having multiple conversations with faculty, staff, and students to gain a sense of the inner workings and whether it is a good personal fit. Students concerned about being the only Black student, or one of a very small number, might also want to investigate the racial composition of the program and institution overall—both for students and faculty.

2) **Know the funding options**. A student may want to apply for an assistantship or fellowship, if they are available. The student should also investigate what other scholarship or grant monies are available through the institution or department, and the student should conduct broader searches for external money at Web sites such as Pathways to Science (http://www.pathwaystoscience.org/), which houses an extensive funding database. Graduating with student loan debt should be the last resort.

3) **Ask about support services for graduate students**. In Chapter Four, we listed examples of institutional support services that can assist with first-year success. Graduate students should ensure that they are taking advantage of all institutional supports as well, including advising, disability services, mentoring or other support programs, and the availability of funding for travel to conferences. Students taking advantage of institutional supports are often the strongest students who seek an edge.

4) **Ensure the program course work aligns with areas of interest**. The best institution is the one that provides the best fit for a student. An institution may be renowned, but if the program does not offer course work aligned with a student's interest, then that program should not be among a student's options.

Moreover, students should inquire whether they will have the option of engaging in multidisciplinary or interdisciplinary course work.

5) **Select the right graduate advisor**. In Chapter Five, we discussed the various roles of an undergraduate advisor. Graduate students also have advisors, and the right advisor can contribute a great deal to the student's academic and overall experience while in their program, as we have already highlighted. Students might ask explicitly which model of advising is used in a department, or students may at least seek to identify the generally favored approach through informal conversations with faculty and other students. If a program favors a hands-off model, but the student prefers a more personalized approach, the student should take this potential disconnect into consideration due to the anxiety it may cause.

6) **Get organized**. Organization is essential. In Chapter Four, we discussed the importance of time management for balancing the multiple and conflicting demands associated with undergraduate school. When adding the process of preparing for graduate school to one's list of tasks—which, again, should begin well before senior year—the need for a well-maintained calendar increases exponentially. Disorganized students can expect failure because they have designed their lives such that success will be merely accidental.

Of note, this discussion on preparation for graduate school is an appropriate point to highlight how attending a historically Black college or university (HBCU) might provide a Black STEM student with an advantage over attending a predominately White institution (PWI). Some research suggests that attending an HBCU is not significantly related to graduate school attendance in general. However, the data suggest a different picture for STEM majors: HBCUs have an undeniably distinguished and proven record of sending Black students from undergraduate to graduate school in STEM disciplines. For example, during the recent period from 2002 to 2011, the top 10 undergraduate schools of origin for Black students who went on to earn a doctorate in science or engineering were HBCUs (Carter, 2014). The following were also on the list (number of Black graduates who went on to earn science or engineering doctoral degrees in parentheses): Howard University (220), Spelman College (175), Florida A&M University (154), Hampton University (150), Xavier University of Louisiana (126), Morehouse College (106), Morgan State University (102), North Carolina A&T State University (102), Southern University and A&M College (100), and Tuskegee University (80). The role of HBCUs for producing Black students who go on to earn an advanced STEM degree is indisputable when viewed through the lens of data.

Specific HBCUs also have developed reputations for preparing Black undergraduate students in niche ways. We offer three illustrations here, although there are many more. Morgan State University in Baltimore, Maryland, is renowned for being at the top of baccalaureate-granting institutions in America for PhDs in engineering. Xavier University of Louisiana in New Orleans has long been the nation's top producer of Black students who go on to earn a medical degree. Its record is superior even to Ivy League schools such as Harvard University. Fisk University in Nashville, Tennessee, has a formal partnership with the highly regarded Vanderbilt University, located in the same city. The Fisk-Vanderbilt Master's-to-PhD Bridge Program, partnership provides a conduit of opportunity for students. Additionally, we can also highlight Spelman College, which has a long history of preparing Black females for STEM careers, and we can point to the fact that one study showed 17 of the top 20 producers of Black STEM degrees were HBCUs (Borden & Brown, 2004). Black students who select an HBCU for their undergraduate STEM education can expect an unmatched level of preparation for graduate school with opportunities to match.

SUCCEEDING IN GRADUATE SCHOOL

Once in graduate school, STEM students can do many things to succeed. Most strategies already covered in this book also apply to graduate students, especially as they relate to overcoming racial barriers. The racial composition of many STEM graduate schools is such that Black students can easily feel marginalized and demoralized, as well as expend a great deal of energy wondering whether they are receiving fair treatment due to their race. We encourage students to review Chapters Four and Five for ways they can prepare to encounter and overcome race-based barriers. At the same time, a student should understand that graduate school is a very different environment compared to undergraduate school. Therefore, to the strategies already outlined in prior chapters, we can add several more.

First, a graduate student should focus on transitioning from being a pupil to being a colleague both to the student's peers and to the student's professors. This does not mean a student rejects mentorship and critical feedback from professors. In fact, the opposite is the case. In the real world, among colleagues, receiving mentorship and critical feedback from persons in authority or those with greater experience is paramount to success. The difference between a pupil and a colleague is found in a general mind-set toward one's place and ability, that is, taking on the belief and behavior that one is an emerging expert in their field.

Stated differently, this is a time when the student makes a full transition to behaving as an adult among adults. With maturity, the student should also recognize and avoid getting into dysfunctional or unethical mentoring relationships, which many students face in graduate school. In addition, graduate students need to be prepared for the strong possibility that faculty will simply be too busy or inaccessible to provide the level of mentoring they had promised. This is another reason speaking with current students during the preenrollment investigation process is important because they can help a student separate myths and promises about the program from reality.

Second, a graduate student should be prepared to give an answer at all times. Graduate class sizes tend to be smaller. Relationships with advisors at the graduate level tend to be deeper. Where undergraduate students might be able to escape "under the radar," graduate students can expect to be put on the spot at any time. This does not mean students always have the correct answer, but they should always have a reasonable, logical, informed attempt at an answer. Evading challenges is not a tactic for success in graduate school.

Third, a graduate student should prepare for even less socializing than an undergraduate student. Although collaboration is an integral part of some graduate programs in science and engineering especially, and collaboration has been identified as an important factor in graduate student adjustment and fulfillment for minority students especially, much of a graduate student's time will be devoted to independent research related to his or her thesis or dissertation. This is true especially in the culminating stages. To finish in a timely fashion, students will need to spend a great deal of time working alone, but they should embrace this season as a rite of passage to the elite ranks of advanced degree holders. Graduate students who have trouble transitioning to this independent, self-starting approach to research report extra levels of challenge.

Fourth, a graduate student should learn to work smartly. One of the best ways a graduate student can do this is by focusing as many papers and projects as possible on the same topic, theme, or problem. Over time, students will accumulate tremendous knowledge about their area of focus. Although students cannot submit an identical project for multiple classes (that could lead to expulsion), they can integrate their work to address various aspects of an issue through different assignments.

Fifth, a graduate student learns how to craft good questions. As a graduate student builds knowledge through advanced reading and discussions, the student will discover the so-called "gaps" in the literature or areas of greatest need in the field. Likewise, the student will learn to take very little at face value and instead interrogate assumptions, data, and conclusions by asking powerful questions.

Sixth, a graduate student should continue to build interdisciplinary expertise. Top graduate students can build advanced knowledge in their specific field while also understanding and integrating diverse knowledge from other fields. This knowledge can be built formally through courses or informally through one's own reading, but it should lead to creative integration in actual projects.

Finally, a graduate student—especially at the PhD level—should seek to publish in an academic journal. Students who publish during their PhD studies are more likely to enjoy greater research production and productivity compared to those who do not publish (Horta & Santos, 2016). This challenge may seem insurmountable given the other demands associated with earning a terminal degree. However, if the other preceding recommendations are practiced, this recommendation to publish becomes quite doable.

As noted earlier, many other tips and strategies for graduate school are available through a variety of sources beyond this chapter. Graduate students should stay fresh by reading tips from a variety of sources and by observing and emulating the behaviors of successful colleagues. Over time, the student will develop a pattern of practices that work. Table 6.1 summarizes our recommendations related to continuing on to graduate school.

Table 6.1   Key Recommendations Related to Continuing on to Graduate School

Strategic participation in preparatory activities (e.g., research conferences)
Maintaining academic focus and priorities
Investigating and networking with prospective graduate STEM programs
Locating funding sources to include research assistantships and fellowships
Preparing for race-based challenges
Taking on a professional "colleague" mentality

CONCLUDING THOUGHTS

In this chapter, we discussed continuing on to graduate school in STEM. For Blacks as individuals and as a population to make significant progress toward proper representation in STEM fields, greater numbers of successful Black graduate students in STEM programs are needed. We encouraged students regarding ways to prepare for graduate school, including identifying a program. In addition, we covered strategies for success in a graduate STEM program. Although similarities exist between undergraduate and graduate school, the additional requirements of graduate school are profound. Black students who want to excel must be prepared to navigate the complexities of the STEM workforce. In the next chapter, we will discuss how students can best prepare and navigate the complexities of the STEM workforce.

CHAPTER SEVEN

Choosing a Career in STEM

Advances in science, technology, engineering, and mathematics (STEM) have long been central to our nation's ability to manufacture better and smarter products, improve health care, develop cleaner and more efficient domestic energy sources, preserve the environment, safeguard national security, and grow the economy. During this era of educational reform, STEM education has become a critical part of preparing students for the diversifying occupational needs of the 21st century. According to Rothwell (2013), approximately 26 million U.S. jobs require a significant amount of STEM knowledge or skill in at least one of the designated areas. National attention has focused on three distinct areas in STEM: building an educational pipeline from early grade school through college, educating students to improve academic skills, and providing access and support for underrepresented students to pursue STEM careers. In recent years, government, academic, and industry leaders have all indicated that increasing the STEM workforce is a top concern of all the sectors. Organizations such the National Academy of Sciences, National Academy of Engineering, and the Institute of Medicine have all stressed that STEM careers are "high-quality, knowledge-intensive jobs . . . that lead to discovery and new technology" (Committee on Prospering in the Global Economy & Committee on Science, Engineering, and Public Policy, 2007, p. 1). Much like choosing a postsecondary institution to attend, *fit*—or the congruency between personality and career choice—remains a critical point to consider. It is vital for students in high school and postsecondary education to think about how to navigate the STEM career pathway and, more importantly, whether STEM is the best fit for their career selection.

According to U.S. Census Bureau (2008) projections, the populations of minority ethnic groups are expected to increase rapidly in the next 40 years. The Bureau estimated that, by the year 2050, minority groups would comprise 50 percent of the U.S. population, whereas the proportion of Americans classified as White will decrease. Unfortunately, there remains a gap in the number of underrepresented student populations, especially Black students, who participate and successfully complete STEM degree programs (National Action Council for Minorities in Engineering, 2013; Palmer, Davis, & Hilton, 2009). The increased demand for diverse professionals in STEM fields is projected to outpace the supply of trained workers and professionals. Tables 7.1 and 7.2 further illustrate the need to increase access and opportunities to STEM careers for Black students.

The President's Council of Advisors on Science and Technology (2012) indicates that greater attention needs to be paid to the STEM career pathway because there will be an estimated one million fewer STEM graduates over the next decade. Now more than ever, it is vital to reduce educational inequalities that continue to decrease opportunities for college degree completion, especially in the STEM disciplines. Student interest in pursuing STEM degrees has declined significantly compared to the historical U.S. benchmark. For instance, fewer than 6 percent of high school seniors in 2013 planned to pursue engineering college degrees, down 36 percent from a decade earlier (Baum, Ma, & Payea, 2013).

Furthermore, the literature reports a gap between technological job growth and the lack of STEM focus placed on inner-city schools. For instance, according to Noguera (2003), little attention is placed on the positive academic experiences of Black males in postsecondary educational environments. Levin, Belfield, Muennig, and Rouse (2007) noted that in 2002, Black males ages 26–30 on average had 0.72 fewer years of education than their White male counterparts. Black males account for 4.3 percent of the total enrollment at four-year higher education institutions in the United States—ironically, the same rate as in 1976 (Harper, 2006; Strayhorn, 2008). Some assumptions about the status of education for Black students in the United States are apparent based on data that support the idea of an "educational gap," specifically in STEM degree attainment. Students who report early expectations for a career in science are much more likely to complete a college degree in a STEM field than students without those expectations. This suggests that early exposure to science topics, at middle grades or below, may be important for a student's future career aspirations. These interventions might provide opportunities for Black students to participate in STEM programs. As illustrated in Table 7.3, Black students received only 9 percent of all degrees conferred in science and engineering in 2011.

As the Black populations continue to grow, increasing their participation in STEM disciplines will be critical to the health of a growing economy and a competitive edge globally. In the past decade, the United States has faced more global competition in scientific and technological innovation from such countries as India, China, and Japan. As a result, in 2009, the Obama administration launched the *Educate to Innovate* campaign to improve the participation and performance of U.S. students in STEM. One of the essential goals for the United States is to better prepare Black students for college, particularly for careers in STEM. Ultimately,

Table 7.1 Selected STEM Occupations with Many Job Openings, Projected 2012–2022

Occupation	Job Openings, Projected 2012–2022	Employment 2012	Employment Projected 2022	Median Annual Wage in Dollars ($), May 2013	Typical Entry-Level Education
Software developers, applications	218,500	613,000	752,900	92,660	Bachelor's degree
Computer systems analysts	209,600	520,600	658,500	81,190	Bachelor's degree
Computer user support specialists	196,900	547,700	658,500	46,620	Some college, no degree
Software developers, systems software	134,700	405,000	487,800	101,410	Bachelor's degree
Civil engineers	120,100	272,900	326,600	80,770	Bachelor's degree
Computer programmers	118,100	343,700	372,100	76,140	Bachelor's degree
Sales representatives, wholesale and manufacturing, technical and scientific	111,800	382,300	419,500	74,520	Bachelor's degree
Network and computer systems administrators	100,500	366,400	409,400	74,000	Bachelor's degree
Mechanical engineers	99,700	258,100	269,700	82,100	Bachelor's degree
Computer and information systems managers	97,100	332,700	383,600	123,950	Bachelor's degree
Industrial engineers	75,400	223,300	233,400	80,300	Bachelor's degree
Architectural and engineering managers	60,600	193,800	206,900	128,170	Bachelor's degree
Web developers	50,700	141,400	169,900	63,160	Associate's degree
Electrical engineers	44,100	166,100	174,000	89,180	Bachelor's degree
Computer network architects	43,500	143,400	164,300	95,380	Bachelor's degree

Source: U.S. Bureau of Labor Statistics, Employment Projections program (employment, projections, and education data) and Occupational Employment Statistics survey (wage data), 2012.

Table 7.2   Selected STEM Occupations with Fast Employment Growth, Projected 2012–2022

Occupation	Employment Growth, Projected 2012–2022 (%)	Median Annual Wage in Dollars ($), May 2013	Typical Entry-Level Education
Information security analysts	37	88,590	Bachelor's degree
Operations research analysts	27	74,630	Bachelor's degree
Statisticians	27	79,290	Master's degree
Biomedical engineers	26	88,670	Bachelor's degree
Actuaries	26	94,340	Bachelor's degree
Petroleum engineers	26	132,320	Bachelor's degree
Computer systems analysts	25	81,190	Bachelor's degree
Software developers, applications	23	92,660	Bachelor's degree
Mathematicians	23	102,440	Master's degree
Software developers, systems software	20	101,410	Bachelor's degree
Computer user support specialists	20	46,620	Some college, no degree
Web developers	20	63,160	Associate's degree
Civil engineers	20	80,770	Bachelor's degree
Biological science teachers, postsecondary	20	75,740	Doctoral or professional degree
Environmental science and protection technicians, including health	20	41,700	Associate's degree

Source: U.S. Bureau of Labor Statistics, Employment Projections program (employment, projections, and education data) and Occupational Employment Statistics survey (wage data), 2012.

by creating a diversified STEM workforce that better reflects the demographics of the population, the United States

will be able to capture benefits such as an increased standard of living, new career opportunities, increased accessibility to programs and products, and economic prosperity. In other words, advances in medicine, enhanced national security, environmentally sound resource management, and economic growth are all indicators of a healthy and diverse STEM workforce. (The White House, n.d.)

Table 7.3   Bachelor's Degrees in Science and Engineering Awarded to All College Students Compared to Black College Students in 2011 in the United States

Discipline	All Students	Black Students	% of Black Degrees Conferred
Science and engineering	554,365	48,341	9
All sciences	1,734229	161,005	9
Agricultural sciences	22,759	575	3
Biological sciences	93,654	6,677	7
Computer sciences	43,586	4,418	11
Earth, atmospheric, and ocean sciences	4,410	76	
Mathematics and statistics	18,021	821	2
Physical sciences	12,888	149	1
Psychology	101,588	11,643	11
Social sciences	172,181	17,880	10
Engineering	78,099	3,097	4

Source: From National Science Foundation, Division of Science Resources Statistics (Table C-14), 2011. Retrieved from https://www.nsf.gov/statistics/2015/nsf15311/digest/nsf15311-digest.pdf.

The National Science Board recognizes the need for STEM innovators to develop new products, services, and processes essential to the role of the United States as a global economic system. The U.S. Bureau of Labor Statistics (2014) reported that from 2014 to 2024, the growth in STEM jobs was three times greater than that of non-STEM jobs (see Table 7.4).

The U.S. Bureau of Labor Statistics (2014) estimated that STEM occupations would grow 1.7 times faster than non-STEM occupations. It is the collective vision on the National Science Board (2010) "to ensure the long-term prosperity of our Nation, we must renew our collective commitment to excellence in education and development of scientific talent. Far too many of America's best and brightest Black men and women go unrecognized and underdeveloped" (p. 1). Other researchers have also warned that the United States is in a state of educational emergency regarding the global STEM competition. According to Callan (2006):

What is needed is a sense of urgency among policy leaders, educators, and business leaders comparable to the policy emphasis that other countries are placing on higher education—as reflected in shifting international rankings. The current level of performance will fall short in a world being reshaped by the knowledge-based global economy. Our country needs to educate more people with college-level knowledge and skills. (p. 5)

Table 7.4   Average Hourly Earnings of Full-Time Private Wage and Salary
Workers in STEM Occupations by Educational Attainment, 2014

	Average Hourly Earnings in Dollars ($)		Difference	
	STEM	Non-STEM	Dollars ($)	Percent (%)
High school diploma or less	24.82	15.55	9.27	59.6
Some college or associate's degree	26.63	19.02	7.61	40.0
Bachelor's degree only	35.81	28.27	7.54	26.7
Graduate degree	40.69	$6.22	4.47	12.3

Source: ESA calculations using Current Population Survey public-use microdata and estimates from
the Employment Projections Program of the Bureau of Labor Statistics, 2014. Retrieved from
http://www.bls.gov/news.release/famee.t05.htm.

For the United States to maintain its global position in the world, it remains vital
for the nation as a whole to continue to lead in STEM innovation; however, evidence indicates that current educational pathways are not leading to a sufficiently
large and well-trained STEM workforce to achieve this goal. Educators must take
a proactive approach in engaging Black students in STEM career exploration and
discovery. In his 2009 speech on the future of leadership in the United States, President Obama said the following:

> The key to meeting these challenges—to improving our health and well-being,
> to harnessing clean energy, to protecting our security, and succeeding in the
> global economy will be reaffirming and strengthening America's role as the
> world's engine of scientific discovery and technological innovation. And that
> leadership tomorrow depends on how we educate our student today, especially
> in those disciplines that hold the promise of producing future innovations and
> innovators. And that's why education in math and science is so important.
> (2009, line 31)

President Obama stresses that it is now a time of opportunity—that we can build
a true "all hands on deck" effort to move the United States forward and address
this challenge (White House, 2016).

While the "goal remains to improve the quality of STEM education and increase
the learning opportunities for all students, there remains an inequitable educational
system based on social and racial divisions. Research has shown that the education system has historically been less responsive to and supportive of the needs of
Blacks" (Harvey, 2008). To create and maintain a competitive STEM workforce,

access to STEM programs and educational support must become an equitable commodity for students.

Later in this chapter, we will outline the various careers in STEM and provide a description of each discipline. Each section is divided based on a particular field of study within STEM (*Careers in Science, Careers in Technology, Careers in Engineering, and Careers in Mathematics*). The other sections of Part III include Sharing Stories of Students in STEM, College and University Directories of STEM majors, and finally a resource guide for STEM support. First, however, the aim of this section is to illuminate interest in STEM while providing a comprehensive understanding of the professional identity developmental process Black students might experience. Data represented in Table 7.5 illustrate median annual wages in selected STEM occupations. Although statistics can provide a rich picture of the gap, this shortage of Blacks in STEM professions cannot be examined solely from statistical information.

To delve further into the idea of why the gap exists, it is important to consider how Black students can visual themselves as members of the STEM community with a strong cultivated identity as a STEM professional.

Table 7.5   Median Annual Wages in Selected STEM Occupations, May 2013

Occupation	Median Annual Wage in Dollars ($), May 2013	Typical Entry-Level Education
Petroleum engineers	132,320	Bachelor's degree
Architectural and engineering managers	128,170	Bachelor's degree
Computer and information systems managers	123,950	Bachelor's degree
Natural sciences managers	116,840	Bachelor's degree
Astronomers	110,450	Doctoral or professional degree
Physicists	110,110	Doctoral or professional degree
Computer and information research scientists	106,290	Doctoral or professional degree
Computer hardware engineers	104,250	Bachelor's degree
Aerospace engineers	103,870	Bachelor's degree
Mathematicians	102,440	Master's degree
Nuclear engineers	101,600	Bachelor's degree
Software developers, systems software	101,410	Bachelor's degree
Chemical engineers	95,730	Bachelor's degree
Computer network architects	95,380	Bachelor's degree
Engineering teachers, postsecondary	94,460	Doctoral or professional degree

Source: U.S. Bureau of Labor Statistics, Employment Projections program (employment, projections, and education data) and Occupational Employment Statistics survey (wage data), 2012.

STEM IDENTITY DEVELOPMENT

The STEM workforce demands highly prepared professional individuals who have a strong sense of confidence in their abilities to perform given tasks. Further, these individuals must be able to solve problems within their chosen STEM disciplines. According to the National Research Council (2014), students must become active problem solvers before they can become an acclimated expert in the STEM workforce. Nadelson and Finnegan (2014) contend "that the confidence and efficacy required to effectively engage at the professional level in solving STEM problems is correlated with the extent to which individuals identify themselves and are identified by others as STEM professionals" (p. 29). In other words, students must be confident and capable of performing specific tasks so they can be recognized and accepted by *other* STEM professionals. They proclaim that it is crucial to explore all aspects of students' identity development processes, particularly as it relates to their professional STEM identities. In essence, examining the professional identity development processes of Blacks in STEM allows for a greater understanding of how this specific student population integrates and engages into the workforce. Integral to the development of a STEM professional identity, students must cultivate their identity as a scholar.

WHITING SCHOLAR IDENTITY MODEL

For Black students, developing a cohesive sense of self is an essential part of establishing an academic identity. Essentially, the scholar identity model provides a frame in which Black students can develop a stronger sense of their academic abilities. To facilitate the use of the model, Whiting (2006) outlined four propositions: (1) Black students are more likely to achieve academically when they have a scholar identity; (2) Black students are more likely to be viewed by educators and families as gifted or highly capable if they achieve at higher levels; (3) the achievement gap cannot be closed nor Black students placed at promise for achievement without a focus on their academic identities; and (4) the earlier the focus on the scholar identities of such males, the more likely there will be a generation of Black scholars who are in a position to break the negative cycle of underachievement.

Whiting (2006) noted that it is vital for educators to seek effective ways to identify giftedness and potential in Black male students. Whiting used nine distinctive characteristic and four interactive factors to illustrate how Black males can develop a strong sense of academic identity. He began his model with the notion of self-efficacy, which establishes the foundation for the other characteristics. Self-efficacy, according to Bandura (1977), is one's beliefs about one's capabilities to produce effects. Students who perceive themselves as higher achievers are compelled to perform at a higher level. For instance, Whiting maintained that a Black student's performance in school is connected to his or her perceived academic self-worth. Whiting proposed that the scholar identity is developed by each of the following characteristics: self-efficacy, future orientation, willingness to make sacrifices, internal locus of control, self-awareness, need for achievement greater than need for affiliation, academic self-confidence,, and racial identity.

Because of the conceptual nature of Whiting's (2006) model, he provided two important caveats concerning the implication process of the scholar identity model. First, he recognized that most of the characteristics might be universal among high-achieving students, regardless of gender and race. However, the racial identity and masculinity components make it more specific for Black males. Second, Whiting noted that the model is not based on the developmental processes of students and is thus not age bound. Whiting further noted that "developing a scholar identity should begin as early as possible and our efforts must be ongoing" (p. 223). For example, Black students' perception of their self-identity might be as a student and not as a member of the STEM community. To complicate their identity process further, others might view their race as a salient factor even if that is not at the forefront of their self-identity. Through the development of a positive professional STEM identity, students are more likely to feel connected to the greater STEM community.

Whiting posits that the development of the Black scholar identity should be a lifelong process that ultimately seeks to combat the various educational and social challenges that Black students might encounter during their academic experiences. As Roberts et al. (1999) stated, students who develop a positive identity tend to have a higher self-esteem, which allows for successful integration into the STEM workforce. STEM careers that have a science focus "are all about exploration and delving into the unknown" (CollegeXpress & Ward, 2015, para. 1). In his address to the National Academy of Science, President Obama (2009) said, "science is more essential for our prosperity, our security, our health, our environment, and our quality of life than it has ever been." STEM education plays a critical role in our nation's competitiveness and economic future. That being said, it is essential for students to examine the different pathways of STEM careers. Moreover, it is vital that Black students self-examine their STEM interest and plan for their success as they explore the types of STEM careers.

FRAMING STUDENT SUCCESS IN STEM

As noted throughout this text, the pathway to obtaining a STEM career is complicated and often requires a strategic career plan. It is vital for students at every level to examine their STEM skill set. Most employers want workers who are able to reason and solve problems using some math, science, or technology knowledge. Some other valuable STEM skills include the following:

- Analytical skills to research a topic, develop a project plan and time line, and draw conclusions from research results
- Science skills to break down a complex scientific system into smaller parts, recognize cause-and-effect relationships, and defend opinions using facts

- Mathematic skills for calculations and measurements
- Attention to detail to follow a standard blueprint, record data accurately, or write instructions
- Technical skills to troubleshoot the source of a problem, repair a machine or debug an operating system, and computer capabilities to stay current on appropriate software and equipment

This section offers students a conceptual map that allows them to visualize their STEM career interest, assess their skills, and then plan for success. Banda and Flowers (forthcoming) contend that Gearing for Success in Motion (see Figure 7.1) is an essential process for students to undertake as they contemplate their STEM pathway. They stress that a student's "aspirations, goals, and desires are the key mechanisms that control the direction of your gears which align your determination to

Figure 7.1   Gearing for Success in Motion (Banda & Flowers, forthcoming)

succeed. It is vital to continually assess your skills as you progress to the career planning process" (p. 2). Figure 7.1 describes how Black students can think about their STEM career planning.

Step 1: "Dream Big." Researchers Banda and Flowers (forthcoming) stress the idea of career visualization. Part of being able to "dream big" is to visualize one's future successes. When dreaming big, students should consider why they are choosing a certain career path. More specifically within the context of STEM careers, does the student visualize himself or herself as a future scientist, astronaut, engineer, or, among many other choices, mathematician? Black students also need to think about *why they are drawn to their chosen major*. For instance, before students can dream big in STEM, they must consider the various STEM majors available to pursue. Table 7.6 provides a list of potential STEM undergraduate majors. It is essential that students further explore each major in the context of the institution they decide to attend. For a degree in science, a student can dream of becoming an astronomer, biologist, or chemist, among others. For a degree in technology, a student can dream of being a computer administrator, a data processor, or an information scientist, to name a few. For a degree in engineering, a student can dream of becoming a civil engineer, a biomedical engineer, or an electrical engineer, for example. For a degree in mathematics, a student can dream of being an applied mathematician, a biomathematician, or a statistician.

Before students begin the process of deciding which undergraduate major to pursue, they must first reflect and accurately assess their skills.

Step 2: Assess Your Skills. Perhaps even more importantly, students must determine whether they are actually good at math and science. A determination in regards to the student's skills should reflect an accurate and realistic understanding of what they know they are good at. Jacobs and Hyman (2009) stress that "under no circumstances should you major in something you don't have the skills and gifts for" (para. 10). In other words, students should be definitively sure that they possess the necessary skills to be successful in the pursuit of a STEM major. Such an acknowledgement should be a viable determinant in the student's decision to pursue a STEM major in college.

Step 3: Plan to Succeed. For Black students to plan to succeed, they must be persistent in the completion of the long-term goal to reach and enter their career path. The result of students' ability to "dream big" and to assess their skills accurately is reflected in short-term incremental goals that ultimately create their individualized plans to succeed.

In an attempt to better understand and visualize the student's plan to achieve a successful STEM career, it is important to acknowledge Blacks who had a significant impact within the STEM profession. The next section provides a brief description

Table 7.6   Possible Undergraduate STEM Majors

Science Majors	Poultry science	Electrical engineering
Astronomy	Wildlife science	Environmental engineering
Biology	**Technology Majors**	Industrial engineering
Biochemical sciences	Computer science	Mechanical engineering
Botany	Data processing	Nuclear engineering
Chemistry	Information sciences	Petroleum engineering
Ecology	Networking physics	Physics engineering
Food science	Telecommunications	Welding engineering
Genetics	**Engineering Majors**	**Mathematic Majors**
Geosciences	Aerospace engineering	Applied mathematics
Microbiology	Architectural engineering	Finance
Neuroscience	Biological engineering	Mathematics
Nutrition sciences	Biomedical engineering	Statistics and decision science
Pharmacology	Chemical engineering	**Psychology Majors**
Physical sciences	Civil engineering	Clinical psychologists
Oceanography	Computer engineering	Educational psychologists

of careers in STEM; high impact individuals found in STEM careers; and types of jobs found within each STEM discipline.

CAREERS IN SCIENCE

Those exploring science careers often ask the following simple but critical question: *What do scientists do?* A scientist is an investigator of the complex nature of the universe or how specific parts of it work. Scientists think about the world in processes; they formulate hypotheses from early observations, and then test those hypotheses with additional observations and experiments in which they can measure those results and confirm or refute their hypotheses. They also observe the world around them, ask questions, and use evidence (data) to answer the fundamental questions. Additionally, scientists identify useful data that already exist or take new measurements to explore different aspects of existing data. Mathematical skills are essential to scientists, as they do calculations and analyze data to draw conclusions about the questions they formulate. The ability to communicate is one of the most important skills scientists have because they must be able to communicate their results so that individuals can benefit from their findings. Through their work, scientists gain a better understanding of the complexities of the world and what factors affect it.

Feats of Science

Black men and women have historically contributed to the advancement of scientific development and discovery. By understanding the scientific accomplishments of selected Black men and women, students can see the essential need for careers in STEM and the scientific impact Black Americans have had in the advancement of knowledge. Following is a list of Black scientists, their particular accomplishments, and their contributions to the scientific community.

Edward Bouchet was the first Black person to receive a PhD in any educational subject in the United States. He received his doctorate in physics from Yale University in 1876.

George Carruthers earned a PhD in aeronautical and astronautical engineering at the University of Illinois in 1964 and worked at the U.S. Naval Research Laboratory. Carruthers invented the ultraviolet camera, or spectrograph, that NASA used in the 1972 Apollo 16 flight.

Emmett W. Chappelle earned a bachelor's degree in biochemistry from the University of California, Berkeley, and a master's degree in biochemistry from the University of Washington in Seattle. He discovered a method for detecting bacteria in water, food, and body fluids through studies of bioluminescence. Chappelle has been honored as one of the 100 most distinguished Black scientists of the 20th century.

Dr. Lloyd Hall earned his graduate degree in science from the University of Chicago and researches food sterilization and preservation to improve processes in packing and preparation. Hall holds 59 U.S. patents.

Mae C. Jemison is the first Black female astronaut. On June 4, 1987, she became the first Black woman to be admitted into the astronaut training program. In 1992, she flew into space aboard the Endeavour mission, becoming the first Black woman in space.

Dr. Ernest Everett Just was a Black biologist and educator best known for his pioneering work in the physiology of development, especially in fertilization.

Marie Maynard Daly was the first Black woman with a PhD in chemistry from Columbia University in 1947. Daly was an investigator for the American Heart Association; she was especially interested in how hypertension affects the circulatory system.

Mary Eliza Mahoney was the first Black person to study and work as a professionally trained nurse in the United States. She graduated in 1879 from the New England Hospital for Women and Children. She challenged discrimination against Blacks in nursing.

Types of Science Jobs

Scientists often work in universities, government agencies, private companies, or research centers. Table 7.7 notes various science careers as well as the subjects needed to be studied in school, minimal education attainment, median salary, and key skill sets needed to successfully perform the job. The careers highlighted show

Table 7.7 Careers in Science

STEM Area	Career	Subjects to Study	Minimum Education	Median Salary in Dollars ($)	Essential Job Requirements
Earth and physical science	Climate change analyst	Physics, algebra, geometry, calculus, English; if available, environmental science, computer science, statistics, political science	Bachelor's degree	62,920	An interest in the social and environmental impacts of climate change, the ability to organize and sift through large amounts of data, good deductive logic, excellent communication skills
Earth and physical science	Environmental scientist	Biology, chemistry, physics, geometry, algebra II, calculus; if available, environmental science, statistics	Bachelor's degree	62,920	Curiosity, persistence, logical and analytical thinking, good verbal and written skills, concern for the environment, love of outdoors
Earth and physical science	Geographer	Chemistry, physics, computer science, geometry, algebra II, precalculus, calculus; if available, statistics, environmental science, applied technology	Bachelor's degree	74,760	Logical, methodical, observant, with excellent oral and written skills, and curiosity about how the lives of people and the places they live in are connected
Life science	Biochemist	Biology, chemistry, computer science, algebra, geometry, calculus; if available biotechnology	Master's degree	84,940	Attention to detail, great logic skills, and the ability to work independently

110

Life science	Anthropologist	Biology, chemistry, physics, geometry, algebra II, precalculus; if available, computer science, statistics, physiology, foreign languages	Bachelor's degree	59,280	Analytical, meticulous, self-motivated, and sensitive to other cultures with excellent communication skills, good physical condition, and the ability to persevere
Life science	Veterinarian	Biology, chemistry, physics, algebra, geometry, calculus; if available, biotechnology	Professional degree (Doctorate of Veterinary Medicine, DVM)	87,590	Patience, attention to detail, good communication skills, and a love of animals
Physical science	Astronomer	Chemistry, physics, computer science, algebra, geometry, calculus; if available, Earth science, statistics	Doctoral degree	95,500	Curiosity, imagination, ability to visualize abstract concepts, and strong math and analytical skills
Physical science	Chemistry teacher	Biology, chemistry, physics, geometry, algebra, precalculus, English; if available, foreign languages	Bachelor's degree	54,270	Enthusiasm for science and chemistry, patience, a positive attitude, observant, with a desire to work with young students and outstanding communication skills
Physical science	Pilot	Physics, computer science, algebra, geometry, algebra II, English; if available, applied technology, foreign languages	Bachelor's degree	70,000	Good physical and mental condition, organized, meticulous, alert, logical, with excellent communication skills and a love of travel and adventure

Source: Data collected from Science Buddies: *Careers in science*, 2015. Retrieved from http://www.sciencebuddies.org/science-engineering-careers#lifesciences.

a breadth of career options that students can choose from if they attain an earth or physical science degree. The careers range in area of interest and focus from a geographer to an astronomer to a pilot. While these careers are distinctly different, the required skill set, such as deductive skills, analytical skills, and abstract thinking, remains an underlying commonality. It is imperative for the student to pay particular attention to the required courses needed to successfully plan for these science careers. As indicated in the table, for example, an environmental scientist must take courses in physics, chemistry, geometry, and environmental statistics to successfully prepare for this field of study. Assessing their academic skill set is a vital step students must take to gear up their career planning process in science.

CAREERS IN TECHNOLOGY

Technologies in STEM include computer and information sciences, artificial intelligence, programming, operating systems, cryptography, and mobile computing. Many universities or colleges teach practical and critical skills that are required to enter the technology workforce such as tasks and knowledge related to processing, storing, and communicating information for computers, mobile phones, and electronic devices.

Feats of Technology

Black inventors and innovators have contributed to the different daily functions of our lives. Although we rarely hear about these groundbreaking pioneers from the past and present, Black innovators have contributed in every field—from ophthalmology to video game development to special effects technology.

Dr. Patricia Bath is the first woman ophthalmologist to be appointed to the faculty of the Jules Stein Eye Institute at the University of California at Los Angeles School of Medicine, as well as the first female chair for an ophthalmology residency program in the United States. In addition, Bath invented a new device and technique for cataract surgery known as Laserphaco Probe.

Mark Dean is an American inventor and a computer engineer. He is credited with helping develop landmark technologies, including the color PC monitor, the Industry Standard Architecture (ISA) system bus, and the first gigahertz chip.

Dr. Marc Hannah is the co-founder, vice president, and chief scientist of Silicon Graphics, Inc., an international market leader in 3-D computer graphics. He serves as the chief architect of the Personal IRIS, Indigo, Indigo2, and Indy graphics subsystems. His company's revolutionary workstations were used to create the special effects in *Jurassic Park* and *Terminator 2*.

Shirley A. Jackson became the first Black woman to earn a PhD at Massachusetts Institute of Technology (MIT) in 1973. Prior to becoming Rensselaer's president, her career has encompassed senior positions in government. She served as chairman of the U.S. Nuclear Regulatory Commission and as a theoretical physicist at the former AT&T Bell Laboratories as well as a professor of theoretical physics at Rutgers University.

Gerald "Jerry" A. Lawson brought interchangeable video games into people's homes with the invention of the Fairchild Channel F, the precursor to modern video game systems. He was one of a small number of Black engineers then working in Silicon Valley.

Valerie Thomas is a Black scientist and inventor best known for her patented illusion transmitter and contributions to NASA research. In the 1970s, she managed the development of the image-processing systems for Landsat, the first satellite to send images to the Earth from space.

Dr. James E. West is a research professor at Johns Hopkins University's Whiting School of Engineering. He is best known as one of the co-inventors of the foil-electret transducer, an inexpensive but highly sensitive device that revolutionized the sound industry. West also earned 47 U.S. patents and more than 200 foreign patents for a range of technological inventions and innovations.

Granville T. Woods was a Black inventor who held more than 50 patents. He was also the first American of African ancestry to be a mechanical and electrical engineer after the Civil War. Woods made key contributions to the development of the telephone and streetcars.

Types of Technology Jobs

Table 7.8 denotes career options in technology. A similar outline devises the subjects needed to be studied in school, minimal education attainment, median salary, and key skill sets needed to perform the job successfully. When students choose to major in and attain a degree in technology, there are various career paths they can follow. The careers range in area of interest and focus from a computer science engineer to a data scientist to a computer programmer. For careers that fall under this realm, the underlying and connecting skill sets needed include analytical, logical, and detail-oriented skills and thinking patterns. Again, the courses that students will be required to plan for these careers include applied technology, statistics, and computer science. Such classes, if not offered at the student's school, can be taken via dual credit courses with the local community college or state institution. Assessing their academic skill set is a vital step students must take to gear up their career planning process in technology.

CAREERS IN ENGINEERING

Engineering occupations require knowledge about math and the natural sciences. The field of engineering involves a wide spectrum of activities extending from the conception, construction, design, development, and formulation of new systems

Table 7.8 Careers in Technology

STEM Area	Career	Subjects to Study	Minimum Education	Median Salary in Dollars ($)	Essential Job Requirements
Computer technology	Computer hardware engineer	Physics, chemistry, computer science, algebra, geometry, algebra II, calculus, English; if available, electronics	Bachelor's degree	98,610	Creative, inquisitive, logical, detail-oriented, and able to work effectively in a team setting
Computer technology	Computer programmer	Physics, computer science, algebra, geometry, calculus	Bachelor's degree	72,630	Good analytical, troubleshooting, problem-solving, and logic skills, as well as attention to detail and the ability to communicate well with others
Computer technology	Computer software engineer	Physics, chemistry, computer science, geometry, algebra, algebra II, calculus, English	Bachelor's degree	96,600	Deductive and inductive reasoning, mathematical reasoning, original thinking, and an understanding of what people want from their computers
Computer technology	Computer systems analyst	Chemistry, physics, algebra II, precalculus, calculus, English; if available, computer science, statistics, applied technology	Vocational/associate's degree	79,680	Analytical abilities, problem-solving and organizational skills, ability to focus on details, an understanding of what people want from their computers, and outstanding communication skills
Computer technology	Data scientist	Biology, physics, geometry, algebra II, precalculus, calculus, English; if available, computer science, statistics	Bachelor's degree	103,000	Analytical skills, mathematical problem-solving abilities, good communication skills, ability to explain mathematical data in everyday language, and attention to detail
Computer technology	Database administrator	Biology, chemistry, algebra, geometry, algebra II, precalculus, English; if available, business, computer science	Associate's degree	75,190	Logical, focused, detail-oriented, and able to communicate well and work in teams

Source: Data collected from Science Buddies: *Careers in math and computer science*, 2015. Retrieved from http://www.sciencebuddies.org/science-engineering -careers#mathcomputerscience.

and products through the implementation, production, and operation of engineering systems. These jobs are often categorized by industry, such as aerospace, petroleum, mechanics, engineering science, research and development, and textiles.

Feats of Engineering

Dr. Baratunde "Bara" Cola is a mechanical engineer, former college football star, and associate professor in the George W. Woodruff School of Mechanical Engineering and School of Materials Science and Engineering at the Georgia Institute of Technology. He was recently honored by President Obama as one of the nation's promising young innovators for his work in the emerging field of exploiting energy transport processes at the nanoscale level.

Dr. Aprille Ericsson is the first Black female to earn a PhD in mechanical engineering from Howard University and is the first Black woman at NASA's Goddard Space Flight Center to hold a doctorate.

Britney Exline graduated from the University of Pennsylvania in May 2011 at the age of 19, making her the youngest engineer to graduate from the school and the youngest Black engineer in the country.

Dot Harris is an energy industry innovator and engineer-entrepreneur. President Obama recently appointed her as director of the U.S. Department of Energy's Office of Economic Impact and Diversity. Harris advocates for the engagement of minorities and underrepresented communities in energy initiatives and serves on the White House Council on Women and Girls.

Lonnie G. Johnson is a former Air Force and NASA engineer who invented the massively popular Super Soaker water gun, which has remained one of the world's top 20 best-selling toys every year since its release.

Lewis Howard Latimer was an inventor and draftsman who worked closely with Thomas Edison and Alexander Graham Bell and contributed to the lightbulb and telephone patents.

Elijah McCoy was a 19th-century Black inventor best known for inventing lubrication devices used to make train travel more efficient. He is also credited in some biographical sketches with revolutionizing the railroad or machine industries with his devices.

Types of Engineering Jobs

Table 7.9 takes a similar look at career options in engineering. Identical to the first two tables, Table 7.9 also offers an examination of the subjects needed to be studied in school, minimal education attainment, median salary, and key skill sets needed to successfully perform the job. Choosing to pursue and attain an engineering degree affords students a wide range of career paths with much availability, given the shortage of engineers in the U.S. workforce. With that said, the careers

Table 7.9 Careers in Engineering

STEM Area	Career	Subjects to Study	Minimum Education	Median Salary in Dollars ($)	Essential Job Requirements
Engineering	Aerospace engineer	Chemistry, physics, computer science, algebra, geometry, calculus, English; if available, applied technology, statistics	Bachelor's degree	102,420	Creativity, curiosity, strong math and analytical skills, teamwork, good written and verbal ability, and attention to detail
Engineering	Architect	Physics, chemistry, geometry, algebra II, precalculus, calculus, English; if available, art, applied technology (CAD)	Bachelor's degree	73,340	Creativity, excellent spatial skills, the ability to work independently and in groups, and outstanding communication skills
Engineering	Biochemical engineer	Physics, chemistry, biology, algebra, geometry, calculus	Bachelor's degree	90,580	Excellent problem-solving skills, ability to work well on teams, curiosity, and good laboratory and mechanical skills
Engineering	Civil engineer	Chemistry, physics, computer science, geometry, algebra II, precalculus, calculus, English; if available, statistics, environmental science, applied technology	Bachelor's degree	77,990	A creative, analytical, detail-oriented mind, and the ability to communicate well with others and consider trade-offs
Engineering	Energy engineer	Biology, chemistry, physics, geometry, algebra II, precalculus, calculus, English; if available, computer science, statistics, applied technology, business	Bachelor's degree	90,580	Detail-oriented, logical, persuasive, and able to present trade-offs in clear language with excellent oral and written communication skills
Engineering	Photonics engineer	Chemistry, physics, algebra, geometry, calculus; if available, applied technology	Bachelor's degree	90,580	Meticulous and detail-oriented personality, enjoys solving problems, excellent teamwork skills, and the ability to clearly state and share ideas

Source: Data collected from Science Buddies: *Careers in engineering*, 2015. Retrieved from http://www.sciencebuddies.org/science-engineering-careers#engineering.

range in area of interest and focus from aerospace to architect to civil to energy. For engineers, the common skill set found among them includes creativity, problem-solving skills, and a detail-oriented mind-set. An engineer, in other words, works with a solution in mind for a given problem. Like degrees in science and technology, there are course requirements that aspiring engineers must take into account in school, including physics, calculus, and other high-level mathematics. Assessing their academic skill set, particularly as it relates to their ability to be successful in advanced-level mathematics courses, is a vital step students must take to gear up their career planning process in engineering.

CAREERS IN MATHEMATICS

While the field of mathematics is the technical foundation for science, engineering, and technology careers, many occupations focus on high-level math skills. These jobs often involve finding patterns in data or abstract logic and require individuals to study and understand the processes of numerical, spatial, and logical relationships to solve problems.

Feats of Mathematics

Benjamin Banneker was a largely self-educated mathematician, astronomer, compiler of almanacs, and writer. He taught himself astronomy by watching the stars and learned advanced mathematics from borrowed textbooks.

Dr. David Harold Blackwell is a mathematician and statistician who was the first Black person to be elected to the National Academy of Sciences in 1965. He is especially known for his contributions to the mathematical theory of duels.

Dr. Elbert Frank Cox was the first Black person to earn a PhD in mathematics from Cornell University and has taught at West Virginia State College and Howard University for the past 40 years. Cox is retired and has established a scholarship to support future Black mathematicians.

Annie Easley is a computer scientist who specializes in designing computer programs that save valuable energy. She has worked at NASA over the past 34 years. She was a leading member of the team that developed software for the Centaur rocket stage and one of the first Blacks in her field.

Dr. Martha Euphemia Lofton Haynes became the first Black woman to earn a PhD in mathematics in 1943 from the Catholic University of America. She has served as the president of the Washington Archdiocesan Council of Catholic Women as well as president of the Catholic Interracial Council of the District of Columbia.

Katherine Johnson has served as a physicist, space scientist, and mathematician and has contributed to the aeronautics and space programs in the United States with the early application of digital electronic computers at NASA.

Charles Lewis Reason was a mathematician, linguist, and educator who, at 14 years of age, began teaching at the African Free School in New York. At New York Central College, McGrawville, he was the first Black university professor at a predominantly White college.

Dr. Dudley Weldon Woodard was a Black mathematician and professor, and the second person of African descent to earn a PhD in mathematics from the University of Pennsylvania. In 1929, he established the Master in Science degree program in mathematics that helped launch Howard's mathematical program as the pinnacle for studying mathematics among the HBCUs.

Types of Mathematics Jobs

Like the previous three tables that disclose career information if students pursue a degree in science, technology, and engineering, Table 7.10 explores careers in mathematics. This table also examines the subjects students need to study in school, minimal education attainment, median salary, and key skill set needed to perform the job successfully. The student's decision to pursue and attain a mathematics degree offers various career options. Such careers range anywhere from an economist to a math teacher to a statistician. The common skill set found among most mathematicians includes excellent, sporadic spatial skills as well as analytical and abstract thinking. The pursuit of a mathematics degree suggests that the student is relatively successful at computing high-level forms of mathematics. Like other science, technology, and engineering majors, those who choose to major in mathematics must have taken high school courses that include, but are not limited to, algebra II, calculus, and physics. Success in the aforementioned courses in high school will help students assess their academic skill set necessary to gear up their career planning process in mathematics.

CAREERS IN PSYCHOLOGY

While the term STEM is used to categorize fields of study in science, technology, engineering, and mathematics, it typically excludes psychology as one of the core disciplines. According to the American Psychological Association (2015), psychology is an essential STEM discipline "because of its direct scientific and technological innovations, as well as its indirect contributions to education and learning in science and technology" (p. 2). Psychology is defined as the science of behavior within the scope of human interaction. In its executive report, APA (2015) has outlined five examples of how psychological science connects to other STEM disciplines:

1. Designing new technologies, including airplane cockpit displays, air traffic control digital communications systems, the computer mouse and other computer interfaces, anesthesiology displays, and redesigning everyday tools, such as the toothbrush, for greater effectiveness;

Table 7.10   Careers in Mathematics

STEM Area	Career	Subject to Study	Minimum Education	Median Salary in Dollars ($)	Essential Job Requirements
Mathematics	Actuary	Geometry, algebra II, precalculus, calculus, English; if available, computer science, statistics, business	Bachelor's degree	91,060	Creative, with outstanding math and communication skills and an interest in business, finance, commerce, or economics
Mathematics	Economist	Geometry, algebra II, precalculus, calculus, English; if available, computer science, statistics, environmental science, business	Bachelor's degree	90,550	Detail-oriented, analytical, persistent, and should enjoy independent research, as well as have excellent oral and written communication skills
Mathematics	Math teacher	Physics, geometry, algebra II, precalculus, calculus, English; if available, computer science, statistics, child development, foreign languages	Bachelor's degree	54,270	Enjoy working with children and be creative, patient, organized, good-humored, observant, sensitive to cultural differences, and have excellent communication skills with children, their parents, and other teachers
Mathematics	Mathematician	Physics, computer science, geometry, algebra II, precalculus, calculus, English; if available, statistics	Bachelor's degree	101,040	Excellent spatial, analytical, and abstract-thinking skills, along with the ability to communicate with a variety of scientists and engineers
Mathematics	Statistician	Chemistry, physics, biology, computer science, geometry, algebra II, precalculus, calculus, English; if available, statistics, environmental science, economics	Bachelor's degree	73,880	Curious, detail-oriented, and able to find patterns and relationships within raw data, thanks to excellent analytical, logic, and communication skills

Source: Data collected from Science Buddies: *Careers in math and computer science*, 2015. Retrieved from http://www.sciencebuddies.org/science-engineering-careers#mathcomputerscience.

2. Promoting public safety with innovations such as the centered high-mounted brake light, which has been mandated on all passenger cars made since 1985 due to its life-saving effects;

3. Improving public health with basic and applied research leading to effective smoking cessation interventions, techniques for improving medication adherence, and activities to maintain cognitive vitality in aging;

4. Introducing new statistical techniques that are widely used in other fields, contribute to applied mathematics, and advance understanding of complex social behavior and decision-making; and

5. Developing educational techniques that facilitate students' mathematical and scientific learning and that help people address everyday problems by enhancing analytical skills, scientific literacy, and problem-solving strategies.

For Black college students, psychology has been one of the primary undergraduate majors. The U.S. Department of Education (2000) indicated that psychology continues to be in the top five majors that students select with business being the most common degree conferred. Maton, Kohout, Wicherski, Leary, and Vinokurov (2006) noted that the increase in the number of Black undergraduate psychology majors could contribute to the improved quality of student support services, new perceptions toward social issues, and a greater value placed on equity within the field of psychology. Unfortunately, there still remains a lack of representation of Black students in bachelor degree programs in psychology. The U.S. Department of Education (2000) reported that 114,450 bachelor degrees in psychology were conferred in 2013. Based on those numbers, females represented 77 percent of the degrees awarded. The breakdown indicated that 63 percent of the degrees were awarded to White females, whereas 10 percent were awarded to Black females. As for their male counterparts, 15 percent of the degrees were awarded to White males versus 3 percent of the degrees awarded to Black males. The aforementioned statistics illustrate the gap in psychology degree attainment of majority men and women to their Black counterparts.

Careers in psychology allow students to use scientific processes, logic, and critical-thinking skills to explore basic principles of human behavior (biological, developmental, mental disorder-related, social). This area of study prepares students for a variety of career field areas, such as business, counseling, health services, marketing, law, sales, and teaching. Psychologists are frequently innovators, evolving new approaches from creating knowledge to meet the changing needs of the world they live in. Psychologists need to have proficient skills in active communication, information gathering, interpersonal management, research, and critical thinking.

Feats of Psychology

Dr. Herman George Canady was the first psychologist to examine the role of the race of the examiner as a bias factor in IQ testing. His master's thesis discussed the role of the examiner's race in establishing testing rapport and provided recommendations for establishing an adequate testing environment in which Black students could academically succeed.

Dr. Kenneth Bancroft Clark was the first Black president of the APA. His work was essential in the famous Supreme Court case *Brown v. Board of Education*. In addition, his seminal "Doll Study" illustrated that children showed preference for White dolls from as early as three years old. Thus, he concluded that segregation was psychologically damaging, which played a role in the Supreme Court decision in outlawing segregation.

Dr. Mamie Phipps Clark showed, through her work with children, that Black children became aware of their racial identity at about three years old. Many of the children in her study began to reflect and internalize the views that society held about them. She also found that many Black children who were tested and informed that they had a learning disability or were disabled were diagnosed incorrectly due to bias.

Dr. Inez Beverly Prosser was the first Black woman to receive her PhD in psychology. Her research examined the academic development of Black children in mixed and segregated schools. Her findings showed that Black children fared better socially and academically in segregated schools. Specifically, she found that Black children from integrated schools experienced more social maladjustment and felt less secure, which was a barrier to their learning.

Dr. Beverly Daniel Tatum is known for her expertise in race relations and for being a leader in higher education student development. Her book, *Why Are All the Black Kids Sitting Together in the Cafeteria?* examines the development of racial identity. Tatum's areas of research include racial identity development and the role of race in the classroom.

Dr. Robert Lee Williams II was a founding member of the National Association of Black Psychologists and served as its second president. He created the Black Intelligence Test of Cultural Homogeneity by using Black vernacular and personal experience. He created the term *Ebonics* to refer to the Black vernacular English.

Types of Psychology Jobs

There are many possible career paths as a psychologist (see Table 7.11). The aim for psychologists is to work in environments where they can study cognitive, emotional, and social processes, as well as the behavior of individuals or groups. For psychologists, their work process typically involves observing, interpreting, and recording how individuals relate to one another and their environments.

Table 7.11 Careers in Psychology

STEM Area	Career	Subjects to Study	Minimum Education	Median Salary in Dollars ($)	Essential Job Requirements
Psychology	Developmental psychologists	Developmental theory, statistics, and research methodology	Doctorate	91,140	Developmental psychologists aim to correct behavioral disorders caused by improper development.
Psychology	Forensic psychologists	Abnormal psychology, forensics, and the psychology of deviance	Master's degree/doctorate	74,310	Forensic psychologists typically perform research, administer tests and evaluations, conduct interviews, observe witness/suspect behaviors, document their findings in writing, and testify in court.
Psychology	Research psychologists	Developmental theory, statistics, and research methodology	Doctorate	98,910	Research psychologists conduct a significant amount of experimentation and research. Individuals who have excellent analytical and investigation skills could assist many organizations in the future by providing these outstanding services.
Psychology	Industrial-organizational psychologists	Developmental theory, statistics, and research methodology	Master's degree/doctorate	55,000	Industrial-organizational psychologists conduct research studies of physical work environments, organizational structures, communication systems, group interactions, morale, and motivation to assess organizational functioning.
Psychology	School psychologists	Education developmental theory, counseling, and research methodology	Doctorate	68,900	School psychologists work in elementary and secondary schools or school district offices to resolve students' learning and behavior problems. School psychologists are trained in both education and psychology.

Source: Data collected from U.S. Department of Labor, Bureau of Labor Statistics, 2015. Retrieved from http://www.bls.gov/ooh/life-physical-and-social-science/psychologists.htm.

Table 7.12   Key Recommendations Related to Choosing a STEM Career

Reviewing needs and values as they relate to professional/academic development and STEM career awareness

Checking knowledge and understanding of different STEM careers to ensure awareness of a wide range of STEM pathways that are available

Understanding the market demands for different STEM careers in order to find employment after education is complete

Knowing STEM history and understanding the impact of Black leaders in STEM in order to connect to the chosen STEM profession

CONCLUDING THOUGHTS

In this chapter, we focused on providing the reader with information related to choosing a STEM career. This chapter offered the reader a critical and practical examination of STEM careers, course requirements, minimal education, median salary, and key skill sets required for success in STEM. We also offered additional information about important Black innovators and leaders in different STEM fields to help raise awareness of the impact Black women and men have had on STEM-related careers. Lastly, we offered the reader a snapshot look at what career options are available to students *if* they *choose* to pursue STEM career aspirations. The next chapter, *Sharing Stories*, focuses on personal testimonies from real STEM students and professionals.

CHAPTER EIGHT

Sharing Stories

The previous chapters illustrated via the use of data that there continues to be a shortage of STEM professionals within the United States, specifically as it relates to Blacks. Moreover, we detailed the importance of the development of a scholar identity model and the need to plan for a success in STEM. We also identified key Black men and women who made a significant contribution as STEM professionals. To amplify the latter, this chapter focuses on the shared narratives of contemporary Black men and women and their respective experiences in the STEM pipeline as well as career trajectories.

TAISHA BOWMAN

Taisha Bowman is currently a fourth-year chemistry education student at the University of Maryland, Baltimore County. Upon her graduation in May 2017, she will receive a Bachelor of Arts in chemistry and a Secondary Education Certification. With her degree, she will become a high school chemistry teacher in underprivileged and underserved areas. She is going to teach in various underserved areas across the United States so to develop a holistic understanding of the community that she wants to serve. After she has gained the understanding that she is looking for, she will pursue a PhD in education policy so that she can create policies that not only help all students become scholars but also help all teachers develop and create scholars.

During my childhood, I was never interested in science, technology, engineering, and mathematics (STEM). I just wanted to travel the world and draw. I believed this would be my destiny until the sixth grade when surprisingly, I started to fail science. Failing was new to me as I had never failed anything before, nor had I gotten anything below an A. After receiving my first progress report that stated I was failing, I went home crying because I knew I was in trouble for not maintaining a strong academic record; failure was not acceptable in my house. To fix my grade, I had to participate in the science fair because my teacher made it an extra credit opportunity worth 20 points, which would pull my grade up two letters.

I had no idea what to do because I had very little motivation to delve into science. The subject didn't seem like fun to me, but I knew I had to do something. I went home and looked around the house. I looked for anything that I found interesting and was science related. I did not want to do something that I could find on a "Science Projects for Kids" Web site. I wanted to come up with something on my own because I knew I would be more interested. Unfortunately, I could not find anything that interested me.

I decided that I would eat my dinner before I retreated to the "Science Projects for Kids" Web site for ideas. As I looked in the fridge for my dinner, I noticed cheese with mold on it. For some reason, this moldy cheese piqued my interest. I thought to myself, "Why is it that cheese gets moldy? What does the fridge do to keep it from getting moldy so fast?" Just like that, I had begun my scientific process for my science fair project.

I enjoyed researching a way to test and model my hypothesis. I also enjoyed finding other people who had similar thoughts and experiments as me. This process was like a puzzle to me, and if there was anything I loved to do when I was a kid, it was puzzles. My project ended up going to the regional science fair where I got an honorary mention and got to see science projects from many students. I was so impressed with all the things that I saw, all the ways people were testing their own hypotheses, and how encouraging everyone was. It was from then on that I fell in love with STEM.

I was so in love with STEM that I started signing up to participate in STEM-related programs. For example, in 2008, I attended a summer camp at George Mason University where kids got to explore science and art. From 2009 to 2011, I was involved in the Pre-College Science Scholars Academy at Bowie State University, where high school students took college courses and lived on campus for free for three summers. During the 2010–2011 school year, I participated in a dual-enrollment program with Prince George's Community College where I gained college credit for forensic science and environmental science. During the 2011–2012 school year, I enrolled in another dual-enrollment program with University of Maryland, College Park, and earned college credit for a mathematics for engineers class. Throughout all of high school, I was an honors student and a science and technology student. I even graduated with the highest amount of college credits earned in Prince George's County, Maryland, in 2012. I was determined to be as well-versed as I possibly could be in STEM. While I immersed myself in STEM throughout high school, it was not until college that my desire to pursue STEM was challenged.

Finding My Place in STEM: The College Experience

Before entering college, I believed that the pathway for my STEM career was set. However, my path changed when I got to University of Maryland, Baltimore

County (UMBC). Initially, I entered UMBC as a member of the Sherman STEM Teacher Scholars Program with the intention to become a neuroscience professor. I majored in biology with the mind-set that I would be able to support the development of future STEM professionals. Two weeks into my first semester of college, I switched to a chemistry education major. Even though I was good with biology, I realized very quickly that I did not like it. What I liked about biology was the chemistry in it. Later on in the semester, I also realized that I did not want to pursue a neuroscience-related career. It seemed nothing like what I saw on TV, and I had way more fun volunteering with middle- and high school students.

Overcoming the Challenges

When it came to my classes, I always knew the topics down to their core concepts, but I would fail my exams. I would get Cs and Ds and have to repeat my math and chemistry classes. I even lost my scholarship. I had no idea what was going on, and I was ready to quit. I went from being at the top of my class in high school to needing to add a fifth year in college because of repeating classes.

I stayed discouraged for some time until one day, I realized that what worked in high school was not going to work in college. What worked in those dual-enrollment classes was not going to work at UMBC. Something had to change. I studied with different people. I adopted a new study strategy every time I got a grade back that I did not like. I was not going to continue to wallow in my sadness and disappointment. I had to put my pride aside and ask for help when I needed it and before I needed it. I went to classes to help combat my test anxiety. I scheduled weekly tutoring sessions. I made sure that I reviewed everything after class and did not let the knowledge slip away. Next thing you know, I went from barely passing my classes, to being close to achieving a 4.0 for a semester.

Navigating Being Black and Female in STEM

While my grades have drastically improved, I still struggle. My struggle is not a one of material, but more so a struggle with the students I work with in labs. It is not easy being the only Black woman in the class. Sometimes it gets so hard that I wish I never picked my major. Moreover, I have to walk a fine line between standing up for myself and not being "angry." For example, in my Advanced Chemistry Lab, I was constantly put down by my White male lab partners. They put me down and felt more superior to me because of their major. They major in chemical engineering, which is considered the hardest major at UMBC. Because of this belief, I had to prove myself from day one. I had to fight for my input to be acknowledged and then further fight for my input to be considered correct. While doing this, I had to make sure that I did not come off as too aggressive. Every time the tone of my voice was too serious or the look on my face was too displeased, I suddenly seemed so "angry" to them. It was not until my lab partners noticed that my work received As, that they started to listen to me and respect my input.

Since I am usually the only Black woman, I frequently have to fight to be considered a valuable member of a group every semester. However, I try not to let it get to me; I use it as fuel for my fire to succeed. I will not let anyone put me down. I will not let a few people deter me from being an educator. I am in school to be a chemistry teacher, not a nervous wreck around people troubled by isms (racism, sexism, etc.).

My Thoughts

As an aspiring chemistry teacher, I want my future students to listen to my story and understand that it takes more than turning the pages in a book to be successful. They have to work hard for it, they have to find what works best for them, and they have to train their mind and maintain their body in order to perform the best they can. I want my future students to be self-starters, critical thinkers, and problem solvers. I want to give them an opportunity to figure out how they can bounce back if they fail. I want them to have the knowledge and courage to contribute and inspire in whatever field they pursue. It might not seem likely that a teacher can do that for a student, but I would have never considered STEM in the first place if my sixth-grade teacher did not make the science fair an extra credit opportunity.

CYNTRICA EATON

Dr. Eaton is an associate professor in the Department of Computer Science at Norfolk State University (NSU). She received her BS in computer science in 2001 from NSU and her PhD in computer science from the University of Maryland, College Park (UMCP), in 2008. Dr. Eaton's graduate studies were supported with awards from the National Consortium for Graduate Degrees for Minorities in Engineering and Science, Inc. (GEM); the David and Lucile Packard Foundation; and the American Association for the Advancement of Science (AAAS).

Congratulations on your interest in a STEM career! Perhaps I'm exposing my bias, but from my perspective, careers in the natural and physical sciences are extremely fulfilling and provide a wealth of opportunity for both professional and personal growth. That, of course, is the good news; the bad news and hard truth is that many of the students who embark on STEM careers are deterred by the rigor and challenge inherent in undertaking a STEM major. This factor raises a natural question: What tools can students use to stay in their majors and, ultimately, become successful STEM professionals?

The goal of this article is to highlight a very straightforward, yet pivotal approach to successfully completing a STEM major; namely, extracurricular activities. Before we talk more about that, let's take a quick step back. Having a strong cadre of STEM professionals is critical to maintaining national competitiveness, remaining on the forefront of innovation, and ensuring the health and safety of our citizens. As a result, several researchers are exploring not only how to attract, sustain, and graduate STEM majors but also to ensure that the majors who emerge with degrees from our institutions reflect the diversity of the nation. I was a member of a cross-institutional, cross-disciplinary team that linked psychologists from Old Dominion University (ODU) with computer scientists and engineers from Norfolk State University (NSU). Our goal was to understand the impact extracurricular activities have on student persistence in STEM programs; the results were astounding. In particular, we found that across institutional, race, and gender differences, students who participated in extracurricular activities were most likely to be fulfilled in their major and to graduate with a STEM degree. This raises the next question: What activities are considered "extracurricular," and how can students get connected with such activities?

In our study, extracurricular activities encompassed things such as finding a mentor, participating in science fairs, joining science clubs, and participating in internships. In general, these activities enable students to gain exposure to a community of like-minded individuals, to explore topics of interest beyond normal coursework, and to gain a better perspective of how they might fit into STEM as a professional. Most colleges give students a great deal of access to one or more of these activities; high school students may have to be a little more creative to gain access but may be able to, in some cases, link with nearby universities in pursuit of such opportunities. The key take-away is this: exploring, identifying, and taking advantage of opportunities to go beyond required academic activity in order to build a professional network, tap into the wisdom of someone in the field who has already accomplished one of your future goals, and participating in apprenticeships can be hugely impactful. Students should actively seek professors, upperclassmen, and campus groups early on in their academic careers to understand the options they have available and to construct a plan for taking advantage of those that interest them most.

From a very personal perspective, extracurricular activities were a significant part of my high school and undergraduate academic experiences. As a junior in high school, I learned of an opportunity to do an internship at NASA Langley Research Center in a program called the Summer High School Apprenticeship Research Program (SHARP). That experience was critical to helping me establish a draft of my STEM identity before I started college. I chose to attend NSU largely because of the Dozoretz National Institute for Mathematics and Applied Sciences (DNIMAS) program. DNIMAS featured a full-scholarship, a living-learning community in which program scholars lived in the same residence halls and took many of the same courses, and support for identifying internships of interest. Also as an undergraduate, I did internships at the Massachusetts Institute of Technology (MIT) in the MIT Summer Research Program (MSRP) and Kodak; I also did research on campus during the semesters.

All combined, each of the activities named left an imprint on my professional life, my personal life, or both. From friends, to larger networks of interconnected individuals, to important, hands-on learning opportunities, I can look back on my experiences and see how they shaped my life and provided the platform for future success. To this day, I am thankful for the adults and peers I've encountered along the way who suggested I apply for internship/scholarship programs, gave me insight on how to make it to and beyond the next level, and helped provide the emotional support needed to overcome very challenging academic requirements.

With that said, I extend the challenge to you! Actively seek out science clubs, mentors, peers with similar interests, and opportunities to get hands-on training via internships. The connections and exposure achieved from those efforts will likely help you to successfully complete your STEM degree and push you to challenge yourself in ways you never dreamed!

DONOVAN WHITE

Donovan White graduated high school from the Jefferson County International Baccalaureate school in 2011 and received his IB diploma in addition to the traditional high school diploma. He entered college at the University of Alabama at Birmingham later that fall and was accepted into the institution's Science and Technology Honors Program. Donovan graduated four years later with a degree in biomedical engineering (with honors) and minors in biology, chemistry, and Japanese. Currently, he is a class of 2019 MD candidate at Weill Cornell Medical, with the hopes of working as a neurosurgeon.

Growing up in Birmingham, Alabama, you learn a lot about the importance of race. I'm sure it was not a coincidence that every doctor my parents chose when I was growing up was Black. In Birmingham, race is the first thought rather than an afterthought. The irony is that the best opportunities they wanted for me would not always be with Black people. I think this problem lies in the hearts of every African American that seeks success. In our society, much of the money, fame, and resources belong to White people, and as ambitious minorities, we must always straddle the line between obtaining the highest degree of success possible while acquiring further racial and social isolation. This dichotomy characterizes my education.

My family did not live in the most resource-rich area of Birmingham, but they still worked to give me exposure to different career paths. I received lessons in art, piano, creative writing, and even karate. I did not settle on medicine until I was a junior in high school. Before then, I had wanted to be a professional basketball player. Being a tall, Black male largely meditated my decision. Society and my environment told me the NBA should be my future even though I was also a straight A student. At times I was told, "you should be the next president," but for every statement like that, I received 50 more, "you should play ball!" Over time, you begin to believe what people tell you. You internalize the stereotypes about your future, and it makes breaking away very difficult. I played basketball for four years, and I was constantly spurred on by thoughts of the NBA. Never was I told of another career. I once mentioned that I might do nursing, like my parents, but they quickly shot that down when they said it would not make as much money as the NBA.

When searching for a career, it is important to consider the pros and cons. The pros I was told, the cons I found out on my own. When I started looking at the career realistically, I realized several things that made being a professional athlete nearly impossible. My chance of going pro was incredible small. Unless I was a star player in the NBA, I would not be making millions. I would have to retire from the job I loved at 40, far earlier than most other careers. These were my primary reasons for leaving basketball to pursue another career. My parents did not know about any of these cons or still rested on the hope that even if the numbers were against me that I could still achieve it. They were, however, very supportive of me leaving. The rest of my community was not as supportive, and I was labeled as being a quitter or simply just not wanting it enough. Additionally, I was given no career alternative.

Part of me can't blame my community for lacking in support and breadth of career options. Looking under the guise of color, the only fields our people were accepted in that paid well were in entertainment or athletics, and thus all talented Black children would be shuttled into these fields. I remember thousands of conversations where elders in my family wanted their children to marry an athlete or rapper. They would even say their child would be the next LeBron James or Jay Z. I do not remember a single conversation where my elders wanted their child to be the next Neil deGrasse Tyson or Regina Benjamin, even though their net worths are also very high, and their accomplishments no less remarkable. Education just was not high on the priority list. I think this is a characteristic of our society. If you never see people like you in a certain area, you are less inclined to go there, be that a party or a career.

I remember the first time I learned about being a doctor. I had left basketball during my sophomore year of high school, and after receiving no direction from my parents or community on an alternative career, I went to the Internet and found physician as a job that fit my interests. It sounded like a great profession, so I began pursuing it. It was only when I got to college that I realized how behind I already was. There are many things I wish I knew early on about becoming a physician that I later realized my peers already knew. I wish I had known how important research was, how valuable community service was, how much shadowing I would need, and how early I should have started studying for the MCAT. While many of my White and Asian classmates knew their importance and how to achieve them, I struggled with trying to convince my family and community of their value. Neither my family nor I realized at that time that research was essential to being accepted to a good medical school. Community service was also discouraged because it took away from me studying, not realizing that the best applicants had managed to get good grades and a plethora of service.

These disadvantages always summed to more nights in the library, more independent searches for guidance, and constant disagreements with my community over my career. Eventually I succeeded in being accepted to an Ivy League medical school, but I never forget how much more difficult my race and background made the process. As a Black male in STEM, you are constantly aware of your identity as a minority, and you wonder if affirmative action works for you or against you. On one hand, it gives you opportunities to be a part of elite institutions and programs with lower than normal test scores. On the other hand, it makes you inse-cure when given those opportunities if you really earned them. Making it this far in life reminds me that your background is strength and that what you think are your disadvantages can really be your greatest source of diversity.

BRYAN KENT WALLACE

Dr. Bryan Wallace was born in Chicago, Illinois. He attended the following col-leges and gained the following degrees: Grambling State University, bachelor of science degree in physics; Fisk University, master of science in plasma physics; and Lipscomb University, doctorate of education in learning organizations, and strategic change. Dr. Wallace was offered a position as a research assistant in Fisk University's Physics Department upon completion of his master's degree. He served in that position for three years and accepted a full-time faculty position in the fall of 2002. He serves as a physics faculty member and is the director of phys-ics laboratories. He assumed responsibility for the modernization and instruction in all physics undergraduate laboratories, as well as laboratory curriculum. The physics laboratories have advanced from partial to full computerization of data collection, and they have received numerous improvements by way of renovation, organization, and utilization of more efficient equipment.

Robert Frost once wrote the poem, "The Road Not Taken." I have always identi-fied with that poem. It very much felt like Mr. Frost was documenting my life. So few African American males embark down this path. What path you may ask? The path of having a career in a math-intensive subject matter. The path of me becom-ing director of physics laboratories was not a likely one. When I was a youth, I was afraid of math. I performed very poorly in that subject area. I did not know how to do fractions when I graduated from high school. I even majored in political sci-ence in undergrad just so I could avoid math classes. However, I realized early on I was simply hiding from a weakness rather than living my life with some sort of purpose. I knew I had a love of astronomy and aviation, so I changed my major to physics. Now, why would I do that when I knew I feared math? Well, I reached a turning point. I decided to face my fear of math. The path of my being able to excel in math began in remedial mathematics. I was sitting there in class feeling con-fused when we were addressing inequalities. You know . . . the less than, greater than material. I remember my professor, Ms. Gamble, said to me, "Mr. Wallace, remember, alligator takes the biggest bite." I then had an epiphany. I was ecstatic. I understood how to apply the concepts of inequalities for the first time in my life. It made sense. More importantly, it was the beginning of the change in how I viewed myself. I for the first time felt I was smart enough to be able to do math. Though I would never have articulated it openly, I thought math was something African Americans just did not do. Now, this was obviously wrong, but up until then I knew of no African American physicists, astronomers, or mathematician. Thinking Afri-can Americans did not do math might have seemed odd considering my father was an architect. I just thought he was the exception. It never occurred to me that the problem was rooted in how I viewed myself. Nevertheless, this was one of the most important lessons I learned, which I did not appreciate until well into my career. You will never excel at something if you inherently do not believe you are good enough to accomplish it. You will facilitate your own outcome by having low expectations of yourself. It's a self-fulfilling prophecy.

I shared this initial story because it will help you understand my philosophy in teaching and instruction. I never want individuals to not realize their true potential because they have doubt instilled in them of their own abilities. The concept of *Stereotype Threat* suggests that people are susceptible to harboring the negative perceptions that are projected upon them by various elements of society, such as teachers, counselors, stereotypes seen on television, and so on. When I instruct students, I am continuously getting them to work simple problems in math or physics. With each problem solved successfully, students improve their sense of self-efficacy. They start to believe, "they can." I believe every difficult problem is rooted in several principles that are simple. If a student has their basic principles down, they are in a good position to handle the more difficult concepts. Taking this approach, I believe, has been instrumental in me being an effective physics instructor. Too many times, we as educators offer a student generic advice: "You need to study harder." I believe we as educators need to be proactive in answering a fundamental question, "How does the student understand the concept, and does that align with the actual concept?" If I can determine if a student has a misconception of a given concept, I can speak directly to that misconception and dispel it. The student is now in a position where he or she can adopt a new way of looking at it. They can experience what I felt so many years ago when Ms. Gamble explained, "The alligator takes the biggest bite."

So, why would I characterize my STEM career as successful? Well, what is successful really depends on what your metric for success is. I have worked at Fisk University for more than 16 years. In this time, I have had the privilege of engaging many students who have gone on to have promising careers. Since many of those students go on to graduate school in physics or medical school, I feel I have contributed to their body of knowledge that has allowed them to not only be accepted into graduate programs but also finish and have rewarding careers.

If one considers accomplishments as a measure of a successful career, then I would look at what has changed since I took my position as director of physics laboratories at Fisk University. When I took over, I inherited the equipment and laboratory exercises of my predecessor, Mr. Binford (deceased). When I took over, the physics laboratory used analog data acquisition systems that had to be analyzed using an Excel spreadsheet, which was designed by Mr. Binford. Now our students primarily use digital handheld data acquisition systems and a suite of laboratories that are designed to take advantage of the Vernier Labquest Pro 2 systems. This has allowed our students to not only collect data but also learn how to do statistical analysis, such as linear regression. Many students remark how being in our experiments in Physics I and II classes was responsible for them doing well in the General Physics class.

One of the accomplishments that I am proudest of is the co-founding and growth of the Fisk Altitude Achievement Missile Team (FAAMT). FAAMT is a rocket team formed to design, build, and launch a rocket to take a scientific payload to an altitude of a mile. In our first year, we achieved second place for reaching the target altitude. At this time, the rocket team is 10 years old and thriving. Not only do we engage in the competition, but we also engage youth in schools throughout middle Tennessee through mentoring, science presentations, and demonstrations. Research suggests students start to stray from being interested in math and science around fifth and sixth grade. Hence, we believe strongly in showing young students from diverse backgrounds that scientists and other participants in STEM are not always typified by the stereotype. Our team has had many experiences of youth saying, after meeting our members, they believe they want to be scientists. Now, we know not all of those students will become scientists, but imagine how their life's trajectory may have been changed by engaging with our students. Research also suggests those students we engage will have a higher likelihood of attending the institution that made an impact on them at an early age. As I like to say, "The students we engage today are possibly Fisk's students of tomorrow."

I have had the pleasure of serving on several university president-appointed committees, including the hiring committee that was tasked with evaluating our current provost. Serving on such committees give you a good indication of how administration views you as a faculty member. To put it plainly, you aren't put on those committees without being on someone's radar, in a positive way.

As stated at the beginning, this has been the road not taken. Many times I find myself engaging in first-time projects at Fisk University, for example, updating the experiments in the physics laboratory, the rocket team, our outreach program, and so on. I will never claim I have been successful on my own. My department has been supportive of my initiatives. I have been fortunate to have a couple of senior faculty offering me good advice along the way as well. My career has been dedicated to the upward mobility of underserved and underrepresented populations in the area of mathematics and physics. Deep down, I simply want to be there for students in a profound way as Ms. Gamble was there for me so many years ago. I have taken time to post physics tutorials on YouTube covering how to solve physics problems. So, if there is a student struggling in general physics in high school or college, they can learn strategies to help them become proficient in solving problems assigned for homework. As I looked on the Internet, I found many people offering lectures or tutorials in general physics. However, none of the material I found was produced by African Americans. I feel if a student of color can see a person of color engaging in math-related subject matter that they have been struggling with, it can positively enhance their sense of self-concept and self-efficacy, thereby boosting their confidence in being able to successfully engage in physics and math subject matter.

An African American educator in physics has definitely been the road not taken. However, I feel that has been a part of why I have enjoyed my career so much. If I may close by quoting Robert Frost,

I shall be telling this with a sigh
Somewhere ages and ages hence:
Two roads diverged in a wood, and I—
I took the one less traveled by,
And that has made all the difference.

CAMELLIA MOSES OKPODU

Dr. Camellia Moses Okpodu is a plant biochemist with 20 years of experience in higher education. She is the director of the Group for Microgravity and Environmental Biology and the Intelligence Community for Academic Excellence at Norfolk State University. She is a member of Sigma Xi, Beta Kappa Chi Scientific Honor Society, the American Society of Plant Biology, and the Ecological Society of America. In 2013, she was inducted into the HistoryMakers collection as a ScienceMaker. In 2015, her biography became a part of the National Library of Congress in Washington, DC. Camellia is a mother of three daughters, Samelia, Elizabeth, and Koren-Grace. Each of her daughters has learned to invite themselves to their own party—Samelia (a biophysicist), Elizabeth (an environmental science major), and Koren-Grace (an international policy major). All understand the importance of being in their authentic space and operating in their created and not found individual space.

My Space—Created Not Found

As a person who operates in a "not-so-traditional" area of STEM (plant physiology, i.e., agriculture), I often find myself at conferences being completed isolated. The number of women in this general area of study has improved but the number of women of color from the United States and most especially African American is lagging. I have learned to mentally prepare myself for my own space. I have learned that I can invite myself to the party. I can create the space that is mentally safe for me to operate. I do not avoid what is hard or what others perceive as spaces for males or others. I simply chart the course, know the rules for engagement, set my compass, and set sail for uncharted waters. Sometimes, like Columbus, I get loss, but often times I find new routes to places and spaces that I never knew existed. I have learned to be a crowd of one—created not found.

As a woman of color and a black woman most specifically, I have not found it always easy to operate in this space. I often hear the unkind words that people will use to describe a woman who is able to navigate the open seas on her own. But I find solace in knowing that Jesus is the captain of my vessel. No matter what, He controls the winds and the waves. I have learned that I need space, physically and emotionally. I give myself time to grieve, feel disappointed, and be sympathetic. However, I know that I can create a new homeostasis in my mind. I never contribute to malice what can be accounted for by incompetence; therefore, I do not take others people's politics as a substitution for my own opinion—created not found. To help me stay focused in my space and not to get lost in out of space, I have created my own vision statement:

I will work to provide opportunities to the next generation of scientists, especially women and underrepresented minorities, to reach their full potential in the scientific community. I will work to broaden participation and diversify the pipeline.

As I move through society, I realize that the most important thing that I can do is to teach my daughters and others, especially women/girls and specifically African American women/girls, to become their own advocate. Do not ask for permission to have space of your own. It is your constitutional right to have space. You are obligated to yourself to be your authentic self. If you have no problem serving others, and God has blessed you with the spirit of servant leadership, then pursue it to the fullest. If you have a dream that others say is impossible, then dream no small dreams. Create the space in your mind and in your spirit so you can actualize it physically. It cannot begin to take shape if you do not first imagine that it exists—created not found.

As a mother of three daughters, I have never worried about them not having a space in the world. What has bothered me is that they fear that they must seek permission to have space. They each can have their own say and create their own space and most important sail to shores uncharted. The value of having additional space is that we contribute to humanity's real estate. We add women who are confident, not self-effacing, and unapologetic of being who they have been created to become. They create their own space, and they do not have to find it or get permission from others—created not found.

CARL S. PETTIS

Dr. Carl S. Pettis is an associate professor of mathematics and chair of the Department of Mathematics and Computer Science at Alabama State University. Dr. Pettis was the first graduate of the Alabama Bridge to the Doctorate Program. He received his doctorate degree in mathematics from Auburn University in 2006. He is also a proud alumnus of Alabama State University (ASU). Dr. Pettis was awarded the bachelor of science degree in 2001 (major in mathematics and minor in computer science) and the master of science degree in 2003 (mathematics) from ASU. Dr. Pettis is the principal investigator for two National Science Foundation initiatives at ASU, namely the Louis Stokes Alliance for Minority Participation

(LSAMP) and the Alabama Alliance for Students with Disabilities in Science, Technology, Engineering, and Mathematics (AASD-STEM). He is also the director of youth programs for the ASU Division of Continuing Education where he coordinates K–12 educational activities such as the National Summer Transportation Institute (NSTI) and the Summer Kid's Youth College Adventure Program (SKYCAP). Dr. Pettis enjoys molding young minds and working with youth to enhance their STEM aptitude. As a researcher, Dr. Pettis is a published author of several mathematical papers. Additionally, Dr. Pettis was named the 2010 STEM Faculty of the Year by his colleagues and the students from the College of Science, Mathematics, and Technology.

It is no secret that in life, we must all make choices. To make choices, one must have options. To have options, one must make the most out of his opportunities. To have opportunities, one must be deliberate in his or her quest to be successful. I never had a three- or five-year plan in life. I simply never functioned like that. I commend those who can and those who are able to live up to them, but I realized that I was not built like that at the age of 18. Sure, I had and still have my goals, ambitions, and aspirations that I would like to achieve. I contend that if one is deliberate in the pursuit of achieving, he or she will find success. That has always been my approach.

As I look back on my childhood, I am thankful for many of the life lessons that I learned from my parents. My mother was an English teacher and guidance counselor during her career, and she always encouraged me to read from an early age. I was the son who hated this while my brother thrived at it. He was a voracious reader, while I was the less than enthusiastic participant who would rather be playing with numbers. At age seven, she made me select and commit to memory a poem. It was up to me to choose the poem, but I knew she was not going to let me get away with some short, fly-by-night passage, so I selected "Myself" by Edgar A. Guest. In essence, it has summed up my life.

I learned early that I had to be true to myself and that meant working hard in all phases of my life. When my athletic career came to an end due to an injury during my freshman year of college, I took all of my passion for sports and my drive for competition and redirected it toward academics. When frustration and adversity came that same year with my studies, I debated whether college was for me, and I truly found myself. Sure, before the injury I was dedicated or so I thought, and I was committed or at least it seemed, but I realized that I was not locked in on all that would be needed to be successful. I had to find resolve, I needed to build my intellectual curiosity, and I was forced to make the choice to grow as a scholar.

So there I was at age 18 with the realization that all of the things I had said since I was a kid about wanting to be an engineer were simply because it sounded good and because mathematics and abstract thought came easily. I had always loved mathematics, but the love began to fade away when things got hard. What grew though was my appreciation for the subject and what it could empower me to do.

I never envisioned pursuing a doctoral degree, and I barely knew what being a mathematician really meant up until then, but I met several mentors during my undergraduate years at Alabama State University who changed the course of my life. For this reason, I often say that I am the sum total of what my parents instilled in me and the young man that Alabama State University helped me to become.

Once I graduated from saying what sounded good to truly searching for a career that would be rewarding, purposeful, and challenging; I decided that employment in industry or civilian employment with the government as a mathematician was for me. It was a great discovery, but it never happened. To be clear, the job offers came, and as I deliberated over my decisions, my father said to me, "You always said that you wanted options", but I was back to having to making a choice. On my list of options were also offers to attend graduate school. This was the path that I chose. I decided to return to ASU to pursue my master's degree. At the conclusion of that process came more opportunities and thus another choice. This time I knew exactly what I wanted to do. I had an offer to go and work on a doctoral degree in material science and engineering, but I was more interested in an offer to work for a governmental agency. Again, neither came to fruition though. My late mentor and predecessor as chair of the Department of Mathematics and Computer Science, Dr. Wallace Maryland Jr along with Dr. Overtoun Jenda at Auburn University, worked to provide me with yet another opportunity. While I was flying around the country for interviews, Dr. Maryland was making arrangements for me to pursue my doctoral degree in mathematics. Through a fellowship from the National Science Foundation, I was able to attend Auburn University to do just that in 2003.

In 2007, with three degrees in hand and a postdoctoral fellowship under my belt, I was again headed to that job with the government; however, 2007 would instead mark my return to ASU as an assistant professor of mathematics. Who would have known? I certainly did not see it coming. My tenure as a junior faculty member focused on teaching, research, and as a rookie grant writer was short lived. I became the department chair in 2009, and my grant writing ambitions took off as well.

Today, I can honestly say that I enjoy what I am doing. I encourage everyone to live out his or her dreams and pursue happiness with reckless abandonment, but remain focused on being successful. For it is my belief that even if you do not know what your destiny holds, you can approach each day with the desire to be successful, which will in turn cast a glow on the path to your true destiny. I have found that good mentorship is important in every quest to succeed. My mentors, Drs. Maryland, Jenda, Ki Hi Kim, and Mr. John Ivery Sr. provided me with direction, encouraged me to be detailed oriented, and made it clear that I had to be determined in my endeavors in order to fully grasp mathematical concepts. There was a strong foundation in place, which is a credit to my parents, but my mentors helped to build my mathematical character.

It has been common practice for me to describe my path as an example for students on how to navigate through high school, college, professional pursuits, and life in general, but I have found the greatest joy in putting my own personal story on the shelf and working to do my best to shape, mold, and assist in setting into motion the pursuit of success for others. This joy cannot be measured and that is why I know I made the right choice when I decided to join the professoriate. This choice opened up doors to endless happiness for me. I now have the chance to give back, to teach the next generation of STEM scholars, and to make what I hope is my own indelible mark on the world.

CHAPTER NINE

College and University Directories

The goal of this chapter is to provide students with an informative directory of colleges and universities in which they can further seek information relevant to collegiate and professional development within STEM.

Table 9.1   STEM College and University Directories

Science Programs for Black Students		
Institution	**Institution Type**	**Web Site**
Xavier University of Louisiana, LA	Private/HBCU	http://www.xula.edu
Howard University, DC	Private/HBCU	https://www2.howard.edu
Georgia State University, GA	Public	http://www.gsu.edu
Jackson State University, MS	Public/HBCU	http://www.jsums.edu
Hampton University, VA	Private/HBCU	http://www.hamptonu.edu
Spelman College, GA	Private/HBCU	http://www.spelman.edu
Texas Southern University, TX	Public/HBCU	http://www.tsu.edu
University of South Florida, FL	Public	http://www.usf.edu
Clark Atlanta University, GA	Private/HBCU	http://www.cau.edu
University of Maryland—Baltimore, MD	Public	http://www.umbc.edu
University of Maryland—College Park, MD	Public	http://www.umd.edu

(continued)

Table 9.1 *(Continued)*

Science Programs for Black Students		
Institution	**Institution Type**	**Web Site**
Morgan State University, MD	Public/HBCU	http://www.morgan.edu
Alabama A&M University, AL	Public/HBCU	http://www.aamu.edu
South Carolina State University, SC	Public/HBCU	http://www.scsu.edu
Louisiana State University, LA	Public	http://www.lsu.edu
Prairie View A&M University, TX	Public/HBCU	https://www.pvamu.edu

Technology Programs for Black Students		
Institution	**Institution Type**	**Web Site**
University of Maryland—College Park, MD	Public	http://www.umd.edu
Alabama State University, AL	Public/HBCU	http://www.alasu.edu
Grambling State University, LA	Public/HBCU	http://www.gram.edu
CUNY New York City College, NY	Public	http://www.citytech.cuny.edu
University of Maryland—Baltimore, MD	Public	http://www.umbc.edu
Virginia State University, VA	Public/HBCU	http://www.vsu.edu
Bowie State University, MD	Public/HBCU	http://www.bowiestate.edu
Florida A&M University, FL	Public/HBCU	http://www.famu.edu
Morgan State University, MD	Public/HBCU	http://www.morgan.edu
Drexel University, PA	Private	http://drexel.edu
Winston-Salem State University, NC	Public/HBCU	https://www.wssu.edu
Barry University, FL	Private	https://www.barry.edu
Southern University and A&M College, LA	Public/HBCU	http://www.subr.edu
Prairie View A&M University, TX	Public/HBCU	https://www.pvamu.edu
Troy University, AL	Public	http://www.troy.edu
Morehouse College, GA	Private/HBCU	http://www.morehouse.edu
Georgia Southern University, GA	Public	http://www.georgiasouthern.edu

Engineering Programs for Black Students		
Institution	**Institution Type**	**Web Site**
North Carolina A&T State University, NC	Public/HBCU	http://www.ncat.edu
Georgia Institute of Technology, GA	Public	http://www.gatech.edu

(continued)

Table 9.1 *(Continued)*

Engineering Programs for Black Students		
Institution	**Institution Type**	**Web Site**
Morgan State University, MD	Public/HBCU	http://www.morgan.edu
North Carolina State University, NC	Public	https://www.ncsu.edu
Southern University and A&M College, LA	Public	http://www.subr.edu
Prairie View A&M, TX	Public/HBCU	https://www.pvamu.edu
University of Florida, FL	Public	http://www.ufl.edu
Howard University, DC	Private/HBCU	https://www2.howard.edu
Florida A&M University, FL	Public/HBCU	http://www.famu.edu
Alabama A&M University, AL	Public/HBCU	http://www.aamu.edu
University of Maryland—College Park, MD	Public	http://www.umd.edu
Tuskegee University, AL	Private/HBCU	http://www.tuskegee.edu
University of South Florida, FL	Public	http://www.usf.edu
University of Michigan, MI	Public	https://www.umich.edu
Virginia Tech University, VA	Public	https://www.vt.edu

Mathematics Programs for Black Students		
Institution	**Institution Type**	**Web Site**
Morehouse College, GA	Private/HBCU	http://www.morehouse.edu
Florida A&M University, FL	Public/HBCU	http://www.famu.edu
University of South Carolina, SC	Public	http://www.sc.edu
Savannah State University, SC	Public/HBCU	http://www.savannahstate.edu
Spelman College, GA	Private/HBCU	http://www.spelman.edu
North Carolina A&T State University, NC	Public	http://www.ncat.edu
Alabama State University, AL	Public/HBCU	http://www.alasu.edu
Hampton University, VA	Private/HBCU	http://www.hamptonu.edu
Chicago State University, IL	Public	http://www.csu.edu
Stony Brook University, NY	Public	http://www.stonybrook.edu
Tennessee State University, TN	Public/HBCU	http://www.tnstate.edu
Texas Southern University, TX	Public/HBCU	http://www.tsu.edu
Norfolk State University, VA	Public/HBCU	https://www.nsu.edu
University of North Carolina at Charlotte, NC	Public	http://www.uncc.edu
Prairie View A&M University, TX	Public/HBCU	https://www.pvamu.edu

In addition, this chapter provides students with a resource guide to help them learn more about STEM areas of study and to assist students with navigating the STEM collegiate and professional process.

Table 9.2   Online Resources to Explore STEM

Web Site	Description
https://www .sciencepioneers.org /students/stem-websites	The Science Pioneers site provides a good catalog of STEM careers through an interactive format.
http://www .pathwaystoscience.org /whatwepost.aspx	This Web site focuses on promoting education and career opportunities in the STEM fields to underrepresented groups. The types of content posted include program information, news items, profiles, events/conferences, fellowship opportunities, and resource links.
http://tryengineering.org	This Web site introduces students to the world of engineering. It includes lesson plans for educators and interactive engineering-based activities for students.
http://www .discoveryeducation .com//students/?campaign =flyout_students	This site has all types of resources for science, math, English, and social studies. The site also has interactive games, puzzles, activities, contests, STEM career information, and virtual labs.
http://stelar.edc.org /publications/fun-works	This project is a compilation of STEM career development information for middle school and early high school youth. The goal is to create a comprehensive career development resource that is inviting and engages the diverse populations of middle and early high school students to build on their diverse interests and draw them into a range of career exploration options and resources.
http://www.sciencebuddies .org	This Web site has more than 1,000 ideas for science fair projects, project guides, project kits, and detailed profiles of STEM careers.
http://stem-works.com	This Web site includes helpful articles and job information in STEM fields. STEM-Works also includes activities and games that will inform the student about interesting STEM areas of study.
http://www.bls.gov/k12 /index.htm	This Web site provides information on careers that relate to STEM interests, as well as fun facts about STEM careers.
http://www.discovere.org	This site has information on the careers and companies at the leading edge, as well as games, activities, interesting facts, and videos for students to learn more about engineering.

(continued)

Table 9.2   (*Continued*)

Web Site	Description
http://www.exploratorium.edu/explore	This site is an online resource and video library for hundreds of topics in math and science.
http://quest.nasa.gov/events/sci/	Conduct experiments from Dr. D's lab, play the online Problem-Based Learning (PBL) game, or just check out the research rack, expert's corner, or media room. This is a great site for parents, educators, and students in grades 3–5.
http://www.societyofwomenengineers.org	This organization represents women in engineering and technical fields.
http://www.invent.org/	Celebrate the creative and entrepreneurial spirit of great inventors showcased on this Web site through exhibits and presentations.
http://www.definedlearning.com/	Defined STEM takes a cross-curricular approach to addressing the concerns dealing with STEM, using performance tasks, career-based video, guiding questions, lesson plans, student activities, and web resources.
http://www.engineeryourlife.org	This guide introduces girls in grades 9–12 to young women engineers and highlights careers. A section for parent and counselors furnishes background in engineering to better advise students.

CONCLUSION

As a developmental process, STEM career exploration serves as a critical approach that allows students a more complete understanding of the multifaceted process that is college and career planning. As such, the authors encourage students to seek resources to help make well-informed decisions about whether to pursue a STEM major in college and, subsequently, which career path to follow after they have earned their degree.

While this chapter offers examples of colleges, universities, and online resources students may choose if they pursue and attain a STEM degree, there is much more information available about STEM pathways. Recognizing the need for students to continue to explore their STEM-related aspirations, it is essential to note that career and guidance counselors can also serve as a resource. In addition to the resources provided, the authors encourage students to launch their own investigations into other websites or resources that can help them further expand their STEM comprehension.

Bibliography

Adelman, C. (2006). *The toolbox revisited: Paths to degree completion from high school through college*. Washington, D.C.: Department of Education.

Ainsworth-Darnell, J. W., & Downey, D. B. (1998). Assessing the oppositional culture explanation for racial/ethnic differences in school performance. *American Sociological Review, 63*(4), 536–553.

Allison, D. C. (2008). Free to be me? Black professors, White institutions. *Journal of Black Studies, 38*(4), 641–662.

Almasy, S. (2015, April 3). Duke University: Student admits hanging noose on campus. *CNN.com*. Retrieved from http://www.cnn.com/2015/04/02/us/north-carolina-duke-noose/index.html.

American Association for the Advancement of Science (2001). *In pursuit of a diverse science, technology, engineering, and mathematics workforce: Recommended research priorities to enhance participation by underrepresented minorities*. Washington, D.C.: Author.

American Psychiatric Association. (2013). *Diagnostic and statistical manual of mental disorders (DSM-5®)*. Arlington, VA: American Psychiatric Publishing.

American Psychological Association. (2009). Council policy manual: Chapter VI. Organization of APA. Washington, D.C.: Author.

Anderson, B. J. (1990). Minorities and mathematics: The new frontier and challenge of the nineties. *Journal of Negro Education, 59*(3), 260–272.

Anderson, E., & Kim, D. (2006). *Increasing the success of minority students in science and technology*. Washington, D.C.: American Council on Education.

AP STEM Access program. (n.d.). Retrieved from http://apcentral.collegeboard.com/apc/html/ap-stem-access-program/ap-stem-access-program.html.

Aregano, P. E. (2015, December 10). A new world: What my HBCU offered that my PWI didn't. *MSIsUnplugged*. Retrieved from http://msisunplugged.com

/2015/12/10/a-new-world-what-my-hbcu-offered-that-my-pwi-didnt/comment
-page-1/#comment-944.

Arroyo, A. T. (2010). It's not a colorless classroom: Teaching religion online to Black college students using transformative, postmodern pedagogy. *Teaching Theology and Religion, 13*(1), 35–50.

Arroyo, A. T. (2013a). *Enhancing equity-minded institutional self-assessment/ learning: A precursor to equitable and poverty-reducing college student learning and development.* Paper presented at the annual meeting of the American Educational Research Association, San Francisco, CA.

Arroyo, A. T. (2013b). Shattering the mirror: A framework for teaching diverse populations online. *American Academy of Religion's Spotlight on Teaching.* Retrieved from http://rsnonline.org/index506a.html?option=com_content &view=article&id=1514:diversity-in-online-education&catid=84:spotlight -on-teaching&Itemid=1675.

Arroyo, A. T. (2014). A composite theoretical model showing potential hidden costs of online distance education at HBCUs: With implications for building cost-resistant courses and programs. *Online Journal of Distance Learning Administration, 17*(1).

Arroyo, A. T., & Gasman, M. (2014). An HBCU-based educational approach for Black college student success: Toward a framework with implications for all institutions. *American Journal of Education, 121*(1), 57–85.

Arroyo, A. T., Kidd, A. R., Burns, S. M., Cruz, I. J., & Lawrence-Lamb, J. E. (2015). Increments of transformation from midnight to daylight: How a professor and four undergraduate students experienced an original philosophy of teaching and learning in two online courses. *Journal of Transformative Education, 13*(4), 341–365.

Arroyo, A. T., Palmer, R. T., & Maramba, D. C. (2015). Is it a different world? Providing an holistic understanding of the experiences and perceptions of non-Black students at historically Black colleges and universities. *Journal of College Student Retention: Research, Theory & Practice.* doi: 10.1177/ 1521025115622785.

Arroyo, A. T., Ericksen, K. S., Walker, J. M., & Aregano, P. E. (2016). Toward an HBCU-based model of living-learning communities. In C. Prince & R. Ford (Eds.), *Setting a new agenda for student engagement and retention at historically Black colleges and universities.* Hershey, PA: IGI-Global.

Azziz, R. (2015, September 17). How to graduate on time. *American Council on Education.* Retrieved from https://www.acenet.edu/the-presidency/columns -and-features/Pages/How-to-Graduate-on-Time.aspx.

Banda, R. M., & Flowers, A. M. Forthcoming. Choosing a career in STEM: STEM majors. In L. Rendón & V. Kanagala (Eds.), *The Latino student's guide to STEM careers.* Santa Barbara, CA: Greenwood.

Bandura, A. (1977). *Social learning theory.* Englewood Cliffs, NJ: Prentice-Hall.

Barton, P. E. (2003). *Hispanics in science and engineering: A matter of assistance and persistence.* Princeton, NJ: Educational Testing Service.

Baum, S., Ma, J., & Payea, K. (2010). *Education pays: The benefits of higher education for individuals and society*. Washington, D.C.: The College Board.

Baum, S., Ma, J., & Payea, K. (2013). *Education pays 2013: The benefits of higher education for individuals and society*. New York, NY: The College Board.

Beane, D. B. (1990). Say yes to a youngster's future: A model for home, school, and community partnership. *Journal of Negro Education, 59*(3), 360–374.

Berger, J. B., & Milem, J. F. (1999). The role of student involvement and perceptions of integration in a causal model of student persistence. *Research in Higher Education, 40*(6), 641–664.

Bidwell, A. (2015). African American men: The other STEM minority. Retrieved from http://www.usnews.com/news/stem-solutions/articles/2015/05/07/african-american-men-the-other-stem-minority.

Bissell, J. (2000). Changing the face of science and engineering: Good beginnings for the twenty-first century. In G. Campbell Jr., R. Denes, & C. Morrison (Eds.), *Access denied: Race, ethnicity, and scientific enterprise* (pp. 61–77). New York, NY: Oxford University Press.

Blackboard Inc. (n.d.). Who we are. Retrieved from http://www.blackboard.com/about-us/who-we-are.aspx.

Blandy Experimental Farm. (2015). Blandy research experiences for undergraduates (REU) program. Retrieved from https://sites.google.com/site/blandyreu.

Bonilla-Silva, E., & Forman, T. (2000). "I am not racist but . . .": Mapping White college students' racial ideology in the USA. *Discourse and Society, 11*(1), 50–85.

Bonner, F. A., II, & Bailey, K. W. (2006). Enhancing the academic climate for African American men. In M. J. Cuyjet (Ed.), *African American men in college* (pp. 24–46). San Francisco, CA: Jossey-Bass.

Bonner, F. A., II, & Murry, J. R., Jr. (1998). Historically Black colleges and universities: A unique mission. *National Association of Student Affairs Professionals Journal, 1*(1), 37–49.

Bonner, F. A., II, Robinson, P. A., & Byrd, D. (2012). Supporting Black millennial graduate students at HBCUs. In R. T. Palmer, A. A. Hilton, & P. T. Fountaine (Eds.), *Black graduate education at historically Black colleges and universities: Trends, experiences and outcomes* (pp. 119–132). New York, NY: Information Age Publishing.

Bonous-Hammarth, M. (2000). Pathways to success: Affirming opportunities for science, mathematics, and engineering majors. *Journal of Negro Education, 69*(1–2), 92–111.

Bonous-Hammarth, M. (2006). Promoting student participation in science, technology, engineering and mathematics careers. In W. R. Allen, M. Bonous-Hammarth, & R. T. Teranishi (Eds.), *Higher education in a global society: Achieving diversity, equity, and excellence* (pp. 269–282). Oxford: Elsevier.

Borden, V. M., & Brown, P. C. (2004). The top 100: Interpreting the data. *Diverse Issues in Higher Education, 21*(12), 33.

Bradley, C., & Sanders, J. A. L. (2003). Contextual counseling with clients of color: A "sista" intervention for African American female college students. *Journal of College Counseling, 6*(2), 187–191.

Branch-Brioso, K. (2009). What will it take to increase Hispanics in STEM? Money, of course. *Diverse Education*. Retrieved from http://diverseeducation.com /cache/print.php?articleId=12347.

Braxton, J. M., Hartley H. V., III, & Lyken-Segosebe, D. (2014). Students at risk in residential and commuter colleges and universities. In D. Hossler & B. Bontrager (Eds.), *Handbook of strategic enrollment management* (pp. 289–310). San Francisco, CA: Jossey-Bass.

Bray, J. H. (2010). *Psychology as a core science, technology, engineering, and mathematics (STEM) discipline*. Retrieved from http://www.germantownschools .org/faculty/kkorek/Jim_Frailing_Files/Public/20_STEM_Psychology_as_a _Core_STEM_Discipline_APA_Report.pdf.

Brower, A. M., & Inkelas, K. K. (2010). Living-learning programs: One high-impact educational practice we now know a lot about. *Liberal Education, 96*(2), 36–43.

Brown Wightman, S. (2002). Hispanic students majoring in science or engineering: What happened in their educational journeys. *Journal of Women and Minorities in Science and Engineering, 8*, 123–148.

Buick Achievers Scholarship. (n.d.). Retrieved from http://www.buickachievers .com.

Cabrera, A. F., Colbeck C. L., & Terenzini P. T. (2001). Developing performance indicators for assessing classroom teaching practices and student learning: The case of engineering. *Research in Higher Education, 42*, 327–352.

Callan, P. (2006). *Measuring up 2006: The national report card on higher education*. (National Center for Public Policy and Higher Education Report #06-5). Washington, D.C.: National Center for Public Policy and Higher Education.

Carlone, H. B., & Johnson, A. (2007). Understanding the science experiences of successful women of color: Science identity as an analytic lens. *Journal of Research in Science Teaching, 44*(8), 1187–1218.

Carter, J. L. (2014, January 27). For HBCUs, the proof is in the productivity. *The Huffington Post*. Retrieved from http://www.huffingtonpost.com/jarrett-l -carter/hbcus-the-proof-is-in-productivity_b_4665765.html.

Cassidy, K. W. (2015, February 16). Getting women and minorities into STEM fields. *The New York Times*, p. A16. Retrieved from http://www.nytimes.com /2015/02/16/opinion/getting-women-and-minorities-into-stem-fields.html?_r =1.

Center for Women in Technology. (2016). UMBC, an honors university in Maryland: The center for women in technology. Retrieved from http://www.cwit .umbc.edu/about.

Chang, M. J., Cerna, O., Han, J., & Saenz, V. (2008). The contradictory roles of institutional status in retaining underrepresented minorities in biomedical and behavioral science majors. *Review of Higher Education, 31*, 433–464.

Choy, S. P. (1999). College access and affordability. *Education Statistics Quarterly, 1*(2): 74–90.

Choy, S. P. (2004). *Paying for college: Changes between 1990 and 2000 for full-time dependent undergraduates. Findings from The Condition of Education 2004 (NCES 2004-075)*. Washington, D.C.: U.S. Department of Education, National Center for Education Statistics.

Clewell, B. C., Anderson, B. T., & Thope, M. E. (1992). *Breaking the barriers: Helping female and minority students succeed in mathematics and science*. Jossey-Bass: San Francisco.

Cole, D., & Espinoza, A. (2008). Examining the academic success of Latino students in science, technology, engineering, and mathematics (STEM) majors. *Journal of College Student Development, 49*, 285–300.

Collegedata. (n.d.). Paying your way: Financing your college education. Retrieved from http://www.collegedata.com/cs/main/main_pay_tmpl.jhtml.

CollegeXpress, & Ward, T. (2015). Science majors and potential jobs. Retrieved from http://www.collegexpress.com/interests/science-and-engineering/articles/studying-sciences/science-majors-and-potential-jobs.

Committee on Prospering in the Global Economy of the 21st Century (U.S.), & Committee on Science, Engineering, and Public Policy (U.S.). (2007). Rising above the gathering storm: Energizing and employing America for a brighter economic future. Washington, D.C.: National Academies Press.

Complete College America. (2014). The game changers. Retrieved from http://completecollege.org/the-game-changers/#clickBoxGreen.

Conrad, C., & Gasman, M. (2015). *Educating a diverse nation: Lessons from minority-serving institutions*. Cambridge, MA: Harvard University Press.

Constantine, M. G., & Greer, T. M. (2003). Personal, academic, and career counseling of African American women in college settings. *New Directions for Student Services, 2003*(104), 41–51.

Crisp, G., & Amaury, N. (2006). Overview of Hispanics in science, mathematics, engineering and technology (STEM): K–16 representation, preparation and participation. Retrieved from Hispanics in http://www.hacu.net/images/hacu/OPAI/H3ERC/2012_papers/Crisp%20nora%20-%20hispanics%20in%20stem%20-%20updated%202012.pdf.

Dancy, T. E. (2010). When and where interests collide: Policy, research, and the case for managing campus diversity. In T. E. Dancy II (Ed.), *Managing diversity: (Re)visioning equity on college campuses* (pp. 71–97). New York, NY: Peter Lang.

Davis, J. E. (2003). Early schooling and academic achievement of African American males. *Urban Education, 38*(5), 515–537.

Denson, C. D., Avery, Z. A., & Schell, J. D. (2010). Critical inquiry into urban African-American students' perceptions of engineering. *Journal of African American Studies, 14*(1), 61–74.

Development fund for Black students in science and technology. (n.d.). Retrieved from http://www.dfbsstscholarship.org/dfb_prg.html.

Doss, N. (2010, December 10). Best colleges for women and minorities in STEM. *Forbes*. Retrieved from http://www.forbes.com/2010/12/10/best-colleges -minorities-women-science-lifestyle-education-stem.html.

Drake, J. K. (2011). The role of academic advising in student retention and persistence. *About Campus, 16*(3), 8–12.

Eagan, K., & Alvarado, A. R. (2014). "Calculating" return: Using student input data to calculate first-year retention. University of California, Los Angeles: Higher Education Research Institute. Retrieved from http://www.heri.ucla .edu/pub/Using-Student-Input-Data-to-Calculate-First-Year-Retention.pdf.

The Economics and Statistics Administration. (2011). STEM: Good jobs now and for the future. Retrieved from http://www.esa.doc.gov/sites/default/files /stemfinalyjuly14_1.pdf.

English, D., & Umbach, P. D. (2016). Graduate school choice: An examination of individual and institutional effects. *The Review of Higher Education, 39*(2), 173–211.

Erb, N. M., Sinclair, M. S., & Braxton, J. M. (2015). Fostering a sense of community in residence halls: A role for housing and residential professionals in increasing college student persistence. *Strategic Enrollment Management Quarterly, 3*(2), 84–108.

Fenske, R. H., Porter, J. D., & DuBrock, C. P. (2000). Tracking financial aid and persistence of women, minority, and needy students in science, engineering, and mathematics. *Research in Higher Education, 41*(1), 67–94.

Fergus, E. (2009). Understanding Latino students' schooling experiences: The relevance of skin color among Mexican and Puerto Rican high school students. *Teachers College Record, 111*(2), 339–375.

Figueroa, T., & Hurtado, S. (2014, November). *Adjustment to the graduate environment: A focus on URM students in STEM*. Paper presented at the Annual Meeting of the Association for the Study of Higher Education, Washington, D.C.

Flores, A. (2007). Examining disparities in mathematics education: Achievement gap or opportunity gap? *High School Journal, 91*(1), 29–42.

Flowers, A. M. (2011). Academically gifted, poor African American male undergraduates in engineering disciplines: Perceptions of factors contributing to success in a predominantly White institution (PWI) and historically Black college and university (HBCU) context. (Unpublished doctoral dissertation). Texas A&M University, College Station, TX.

Flowers, A. M., Scott, J., Riley, J., & Palmer, R. T. (2015). Beyond the call of duty: An analysis of the effects of othermothering at historically Black colleges and universities (HBCUs). *Journal of African American Males in Education, 6*(1), 59–73.

Folsom, P., Yoder, F., & Joslin, J. E. (2015). *The new advisor guidebook: Mastering the art of academic advising*. San Francisco: Jossey-Bass.

Ford, D. Y., Grantham, T. G., & Whiting, G. W. (2008). Another look at the achievement gap: Learning from the experiences of gifted Black students. *Urban Education, 43*(2), 216–239.

Fordham, S., & Ogbu, J. (1986). Black students' school success: Coping with the burden of acting White. *The Urban Review, 18*(3), 176–206.

Fries-Britt, S., & Turner, B. (2002). Uneven stories: Successful Black collegians at a Black and a White campus. *Review of Higher Education, 25*(3), 315–330.

Gallagher, R. P. (2013). *National survey of college counseling centers 2013, Section one: 4-year directors.* Retrieved from http://www.collegecounseling.org /wp-content/uploads/Survey-2013-4-yr-Directors-1.pdf.

Gallien, L., & Peterson, M. (2004). *Instructing and mentoring the African American student: Strategies for success in higher education.* New York, NY: Allyn & Bacon.

Gallup, Inc. (2015). *USA Funds minority college graduates report.* Washington, D.C. Retrieved from http://www.gallup.com/services/186359/gallup-usa -funds-minority-college-graduates-report-pdf.aspx.

Gamoran, A., Porter, A. C., Smithson, J., & White, P. A. (1997). Upgrading high school mathematics instruction: Improving learning opportunities for low-achieving, low-income youth. *American Evaluation and Policy Analysis, 19*(4), 325–338.

Gansemer-Topf, A. M., & Tietjen, K. (2015). Assessing the "learning" in "learning" communities. In M. Benjamin (Ed.), *New directions for student services: No 149. Learning communities from start to finish* (pp. 79–89). San Francisco, CA: Jossey-Bass.

Gardner, J. N., & Siegel, M. J. (2001). Focusing on the first-year student. *Priorities, 17,* 1–17.

Gates Millennium Scholarship. (n.d.). Retrieved from http://www.gmsp.org.

Gaudet, A. D. (2015, January 21). Secrets to thriving in graduate school. *American Association for the Advancement of Science.* Retrieved from http://www .sciencemag.org/careers/2015/01/secrets-thriving-graduate-school.

General Accounting Office. (1995). *Higher education: Restructuring student aid could reduce low-income student dropout rate* (GAO/HEHS-95-48). Washington, D.C.: U.S. Government Printing Office.

Gibbs, K., Jr. (2014, September 10). Diversity in STEM: What it is and why it matters. *Scientific American.* Retrieved from http://blogs.scientificamerican .com/voices/diversity-in-stem-what-it-is-and-why-it-matters.

Goldhaber, D. D., & Brewer, D. J. (2000). Does teacher certification matter? High school teacher certification status and student achievement? *Educational Evaluation and Policy Analysis, 22*(2), 129–145.

Good, C., Aronson, J., & Inzlicht, M. (2003). Improving adolescents' standardized test performance: An intervention to reduce the effects of stereotype threat. *Journal of Applied Developmental Psychology, 24,* 645–662.

Grandy, J. (1994). *Gender and ethnic differences among science and engineering majors: Experiences, achievements, and expectations.* Princeton, NJ: Education Testing Service.

Greensboro News & Record. (2015, November 5). N.C. A&T remains nation's top producer of Black engineers. Retrieved from http://www.greensboro.com

/news/schools/n-c-a-t-remains-nation-s-top-producer-of/article_41e642fe
-d3f0-5c7c-8614-0a028469f794.html.

Greer, T. M., & Chwalisz, K. (2007). Minority-related stressors and coping processes among African American college students. *Journal of College Student Development, 48*, 388–404.

Guess, A. (2008). A closer look at minorities in engineering. Retrieved from https://www.insidehighered.com/news/2008/05/02/nacme.

Guiffrida, D. A. (2005). Othermothering as a framework for understanding African American students' definitions of student-centered faculty. *The Journal of Higher Education, 76*(6), 701–23.

Guiffrida, D. A. (2006). Toward a cultural advancement of Tinto's theory. *The Review of Higher Education, 29*(4), 451–472.

Habley, W. R., & McCauley, M. E. (1987). The relationship between institutional characteristics and the organization of advising services. *NACADA Journal, 7*(1), 27–39.

Hall, E. R., & Post-Kammer, P. (1987). Black mathematics and science majors: Why so few. *Career Development Quarterly, 35*(3), 206–219.

Harper, S. R. (2006). Peer support for African American male college achievement: Beyond internalized racism and the burden of "acting White." *Journal of Men's Studies, 14*, 337–358.

Harper, S. R. (2009). Niggers no more: A critical race counternarrative on Black male student achievement at predominantly White colleges and universities. *International Journal of Qualitative Studies in Education, 22*(6), 697–712.

Harper, S. R. (2012). *Black male student success in higher education: A report from the National Black Male College Achievement Study*. Philadelphia: University of Pennsylvania, Center for the Study of Race and Equity in Education.

Harper, S., & Kuykendall, J. (2012). Institutional efforts to improve Black male student achievement: A standards-based approach. *Change: The Magazine of Higher Learning, 44*(2), 23–29.

Harper, S. R., & Museus, S. D. (Eds.). (2007). *Using qualitative methods in institutional assessment*. San Francisco, CA: Jossey-Bass.

Harris, F., III, Palmer, R. T., & Struve, L. E. (2011). "Cool posing" on campus: A qualitative study of masculinities and gender expression among Black men at a private research institution. *Journal of Negro Education, 80*(1), 47–62.

Harris, F., III, & Wood, J. L. (2013). Student success for men of color in community colleges: A review of published literature and research, 1998–2012. *Journal of Diversity in Higher Education, 6*(3), 174–185.

Harvey, W. B. (2008). The weakest link: A commentary on the connections between K–12 and higher education. *American Behavioral Scientist, 51*, 972–983.

Hausmann, L. R., Schofield, J. W., & Woods, R. L. (2007). Sense of belonging as a predictor of intentions to persist among African American and White first-year college students. *Research in Higher Education, 48*(7), 803–839.

He, Y., & Hutson, B. (2016). Appreciative assessment in academic advising. *Review of Higher Education, 39*(2), 213–240.

Herndon, M. K., & Hirt, J. B. (2004). Black students and their families: What leads to success in college. *Journal of Black Studies, 34*(4), 489–513.

Hill, K. (1990). The Detroit Area Pre-College Engineering Program, Inc. (DAP-CEP). *Journal of Negro Education, 59*(3), 439–448.

Hinderlie, H. H., & Kenny, M. (2002). Attachment, social support, and college adjustment among Black students at predominantly White universities. *Journal of College Student Development, 43*(3), 327–340.

Hohmann, S. O. (2016). Successful STEM graduate school preparation at Morgan State University. Retrieved from http://understanding-interventions.org/wp-content/uploads/2016/01/Sarah-Olson-Hohmann.pdf.

Holt, J. K. (2006). An evaluation of math and science educational and occupational persistence among minorities. Proceedings from annual meeting of the Eastern Education Research Association. Hilton Head, SC.

Horta, H., & Santos, J. M. (2016, February). The impact of publishing during PhD studies on career research publication, visibility, and collaborations. *Research in Higher Education, 57*(1), 28–50.

Howard University. (2016). HUSEM: About HUSEM. Retrieved from http://www.howard.edu/sem/husem.htm.

Hrabowski, F. A. (2003). Raising minority achievement in science and math. *Educational Leadership, 60*(4), 44–48.

Hurtado, S., Han, J. C., Sáenz, V. B., Espinosa, L. L., Cabrera, N., & Cerna, O. S. (2007). Predicting transition and adjustment to college: Biomedical and behavioral science aspirants' and minority students' first year of college. *Research in Higher Education, 48*(7), 481–887.

Institute for Broadening Participation. (2014a). Finding the right graduate program: A checklist of questions to ask graduate schools, departments, and programs. Retrieved from http://pathwaystoscience.org/pdf/Gradschool_Questions Checklist.pdf.

Institute for Broadening Participation. (2014b). Designing for success. Retrieved from http://www.pathwaystoscience.org/pdf/Designing_for_Success.pdf.

Jacobs, L. F., & Hyman, J. S. (2009, December 16). 10 questions to ask before picking a major. Retrieved from http://www.usnews.com/education/blogs/professorsguide/2009/12/16/10-questions-to-ask-before-picking-a-major.

Jayakumar, U. M., & Museus, S. D. (2012). Mapping the intersection of campus cultures and equitable outcomes among racially diverse student populations. In S. D. Museus & U. M. Jayakumar (Eds.), *Creating campus cultures: Fostering success among racially diverse student populations* (pp. 1–27). New York, NY: Routledge.

Jean-Marie, G. (2008). Social justice, visionary and career project: The discourses of Black women leaders at historically Black colleges and universities. In M. Gasman & C. L. Tudico (Eds.), *Historically Black colleges and universities*. New York, NY: Palgrave Macmillan.

Jett, C. (2013). HBCUs propel African American male mathematics majors. *Journal of African American Studies, 17*(2), 189–205.

Jewell, J. O. (2002). To set an example: The tradition of diversity at historically Black colleges and universities. *Urban Education, 37*(1), 7–21.

Johnson, W. B., & Huwe, J. M. (2002). Toward a typology of mentorship dysfunction in graduate school. *Psychotherapy: Theory, Research, Practice, Training, 39*(1), 44.

Johnson, W. B., & Huwe, J. M. (2003). *Getting mentored in graduate school.* Washington, D.C.: American Psychological Association.

Kane, M. A., Beals, C., Valeau, E. J., & Johnson, M. J. (2004). Fostering success among traditionally underrepresented student groups: Hartnell College's approach to implementation of the math, engineering, and science achievement (MESA) program. *Community College Journal of Research and Practice, 28*, 17–26.

Karanja, E., & Austin, N. (2014). What are African Americans doing in college? A review of the undergraduate degrees awarded by U.S. institutions to African Americans: 2005–2009. *The Journal of Negro Education, 83*(4), 530–548.

Kent, J. D., & McCarthy, M. T. (2016). *Holistic review in graduate admissions: A report from the council of graduate schools.* Washington, D.C.: Council of Graduate Schools.

Kessel, F., Rosenfield, P., & Anderson, N. (Eds.). (2008). *Expanding the boundaries of health and social science: Case studies in interdisciplinary innovation.* Oxford University Press.

Kezar, A., & Maxey, D. (2014). Faculty matter: So why doesn't everyone think so? *The NEA Higher Education Journal: Thought and Action*, 29–44.

Kim, M. M., & Conrad, C. F. (2006). The impact of historically Black colleges and universities on the academic success of African American students. *Research in Higher Education, 47*(4), 399–427.

Klein, J. T., & Newell, W. H. (1996). Advancing interdisciplinary studies. In J. G. Gaff & J. Ratcliff (Eds.), *Handbook of the undergraduate curriculum* (pp. 393–395). San Francisco, CA: Jossey-Bass.

Kuh, G. D., Kinzie, J., Buckley, J. A., Bridges, B. K., & Hayek, J. C. (2006). Piecing together the student success puzzle: Research, propositions, and recommendations. *ASHE-ERIC Higher Education Report Series, 32*(5). San Francisco, CA: Jossey-Bass.

Kuh, G. D., Kinzie, J., Cruce, T., Shoup, R., & Gonyea, R. M. (2006). *Connecting the dots: Multi-faceted analyses of the relationships between student engagement results from the NSSE and the institutional practices and conditions that foster student success.* Bloomington: Indiana University, Center for Postsecondary Research.

Kuh, G. D., Kinzie, J., Schuh, J. H., Whitt, E. J., & Associates (2005). *Student success in college: Creating conditions that matter.* San Francisco, CA: Jossey-Bass.

Kuh, G. D., Kinzie, J., Schuh, J. H., & Whitt, E. J. (2011). Fostering student success in hard times. *Change: The Magazine of Higher Learning, 43*(4), 13–19.

Ladson-Billings, G. (1995a). Toward a theory of culturally relevant pedagogy. *American Educational Research Journal, 32*(3), 465–491.

Ladson-Billings, G. (1995b). But that's just good teaching! The case for culturally relevant pedagogy. *Theory into Practice, 34*(3), 159–165.

Ladson-Billings, G. (1997). It doesn't add up: African American students' mathematics achievement. *Journal for Research in Mathematics Education, 28*(6), 697–708.

Lam, C. P., Strivatsan, T., Doverspike, D., Vesalo, J., & Ruby-Mawasha, P. (2005). A ten year assessment of the pre-engineering program for under-represented, low income and/or first generation college students at the University of Akron. *Journal of STEM Education, 6*(2–3), 14–20.

Lencioni, P. M. (2002). *The five dysfunctions of a team: A leadership fable* (Vol. 13). San Francisco: Jossey-Bass.

Leslie, L. L., McClure, G. T., & Oaxaca, R. L. (1998). Women and minorities in science and engineering: A life sequence analysis. *Journal of Higher Education, 69*, 239–276.

Levin, H. M., Belfield, C., Muennig, P., & Rouse, C. (2007). The public returns to public educational investments in African American males. *Economics of Educational Review, 26*, 700–709.

Lewis, A. E., Chesler, M., & Forman, T. A. (2000). The impact of "colorblind" ideologies on students of color: Intergroup relations at a predominantly White university. *The Journal of Negro Education, 69*(1/2), 74–91.

Lewis, B. F. (2003). A critique of literature on the under-representation of African Americans in science: Directions for future research. *Journal of Women and Minorities in Science and Engineering, 9*(3&4), 361–373.

Lipman, P. (1995). "Bringing out the best in them?": The contribution of culturally relevant teachers to educational reform. *Theory into Practice, 34*(3), 202–208.

Loomis, S., & Rodriguez, J. (2009). Institutional change and higher education. *International Journal of Higher Education, 58*(4), 475–489.

Louisiana Weekly. (2012, July 9). Xavier is still nation's top producer of Black doctors. Retrieved from http://www.louisianaweekly.com/xavier-is-still -nation%E2%80%99s-top-producer-of-black-doctors.

Lundy, G. F. (2003). School resistance in America high schools: The role of race and gender in oppositional culture theory. *Evaluation and Research in Education, 17*(1), 6–27.

Lynch, J. S. (2015). Science for all: A new breed of schools is closing achievement gaps among students and may hold the key to a revitalized 21st century workforce. *Scientific American*. Retrieved from http://www.scientificamerican .com/article/science-for-all.

Maton, K. I., & Hrabowski, F. A. (2004). Increasing the number of African American PhDs in the sciences and engineering. *American Psychologist, 59*(6), 547–556.

Maton, K. I., Kohout, J. L., Wicherski, M., Leary, G. E., & Vinokurov, A. (2006). Minority students of color and the psychology graduate pipeline: Disquieting and encouraging trends, 1989–2003. *American Psychologist, 61*(2), 117–131.

Mattis, J. S. (2000). African American women's definitions of spirituality and reli-
    giosity. *Journal of Black Psychology, 26*(1), 101–122.
May, G. S., & Chubin, D. E. (2003). A retrospective on undergraduate engineer-
    ing success for underrepresented minority students. *Journal of Engineering
    Education, 92*(1), 27–39.
McClellan, J. L. (2007). The advisor as servant: The theoretical and philosophical
    relevance of servant leadership to academic advising. *NACADA Journal,
    27*(2), 41–49.
McClellan, J. L. (2016). Advisor training components. Retrieved from http://www
    .nacada.ksu.edu/Resources/Clearinghouse/View-Articles/Advisor-Training
    -Components.aspx.
McGee, R., & Keller, J. L. (2007). Identifying future scientists: predicting persis-
    tence into research training. *CBE-Life Sciences Education, 6*(4), 316–331.
Metro Early College High School. (n.d.). Retrieved from http://www.themetroschool
    .org.
Microsoft Scholarship. (n.d.). Scholarship program. Retrieved from https://careers
    .microsoft.com/students/scholarships.
Moore, J. L., III. (2006). A qualitative investigation of African American males'
    career trajectory in engineering: Implications for teachers, school counsel-
    ors, and parents. *Teachers College Record, 108*, 246–266.
Moore, J. L., III, & Owens, D. (2008). Educating and counseling African Ameri-
    can students: Recommendations for teachers and school counselors. In
    L. Tillman (Ed.), *The Sage handbook of African American education*
    (pp. 351–366). Los Angeles, CA: Sage.
Morgan State University. (2016). Extreme science internships. Retrieved from
    http://www.morgan.edu/school_of_computer_mathematical_and_natural
    _sciences/internships_and_fellowships/extreme_science_internships.html.
Museus, S. D., & Jayakumar, U. M. (2012). *Creating campus cultures: Fostering suc-
    cess among racially diverse student populations*. New York, NY: Routledge.
Museus, S. D., Palmer, R. T., Davis, R. J., & Maramba, D. C. (2011). *Racial and ethnic
    minority students' success in STEM education*. Hoboken, NJ: Jossey-Bass.
Mutakabbir, Y. T., & Nuriddin, T. A. (2016). *Religious minority students in higher
    education*. New York, NY: Routledge.
Nadelson, L. S., and Finnegan, J. (2014). A path less traveled: Fostering STEM
    majors professional identity development through engagement in STEM
    learning assistants. *Journal of Higher Education Theory and Practice, 14*(5),
    29–41.
Nadelson, L. S., Shadle, S. E., & Hettinger, J. K. (2013). A journey toward mas-
    tery teaching: STEM faculty engagement in a year-long faculty learning com-
    munity. *Learning Communities Journal, 5*, 97–122.
National Action Council for Minorities in Engineering. (n.d.). About NACME.
    Retrieved from http://www.nacme.org.
National Action Council for Minorities in Engineering. (2013). NACME press
    releases: Minorities are answer to U.S. shortage of engineers. Retrieved from

http://www.nacme.org/news/press-releases/41-minorities-are-answer-to-u-s-shortage-of-enginees.

National Center for Education Statistics. (n.d.). Graduation and retention data. Retrieved from http://healthsciences.cnsu.edu/shareddocs/GraduationRetentionDataCHS.pdf.

National Governors Association. (2007). Building a science, technology, engineering and math agenda. Retrieved from http://www.nga.org/files/live/sites/NGA/files/pdf/0702INNOVATIONSTEM.PDF.

National Research Council. (2014). *Developing assessments for the next generation science standards*. Washington, D.C.: The National Academies Press.

National Science Board. (2010). *America's pressing challenge: Building a stronger foundation*. Arlington, VA: National Science Foundation.

National Science Foundation. (2010a). *Classification of programs*. Arlington, VA: Author. Retrieved from http://www.nsf.gov/statistics/nsf99330/pdf/sectd.pdf.

National Science Foundation. (2010b). *Science and engineering indicators 2010*. Arlington, VA: Author.

National Society of Black Engineers. (n.d.). NSBE scholarships. Retrieved from http://www.nsbe.org/programs/scholarships.aspx#.V6uSRJMrLUo.

Nave, F. M., Bonner, F., Lewis, C. L., Frizell, S., Parker, A., McFrazier, M., & Robinson, P. (forthcoming). African American students' academic achievement in STEM at HBCUs: Faculty perceptions on the contributing factors for academic success. In L. O. Flowers, J. L. Moore III, & L. A. Flowers (Eds.), *The evolution of learning: Science, technology, Engineering, and mathematics education at historically Black colleges and universities*. Lanham, MD: University Press of America.

The Network Journal. (n.d.). Lists of historical Black colleges and universities. Retrieved from http://www.tnj.com/lists-resources/hbcu.

Noguera, P. A. (2003). The trouble with Black boys: The role and influence of environmental and cultural factors on the academic performance of African American males. *Urban Education, 38*, 431–459.

Norfolk State University. (2016). The Dozoretz National Institute for Mathematics and Applied Sciences. Retrieved from https://www.nsu.edu/cset/dnimas.

North Carolina A&T State University. (2016). STEM living learning community. Retrieved from http://www.ncat.edu/student-affairs/housing/communities/llc/stem.html.

North Carolina State University. (2016). Minority engineering programs. Retrieved from https://www.engr.ncsu.edu/mep.

Oakes, J. (1990). Opportunities, achievement, and choice: Women and minority students in science and mathematics. *Review of Research in Education, 16*(2), 153–166.

Oakes, J., Gamoran, A., & Page, R. N. (1992). Curriculum differentiation: Opportunities, outcome, and meanings. In P. W. Jackson (Ed.), *Handbook of research on curriculum* (pp. 570–608). New York, NY: Macmillan.

Obama, B. (2009, April). Remarks by the President at the National Academy of Sciences Annual Meeting. Retrieved from https://www.whitehouse.gov/the-press-office/remarks-president-national-academy-sciences-annual-meeting.

Obama, B. (2009, November). Educate to innovate. Campaign for excellence in science, technology, engineering, and math (STEM) education. Retrieved from https://www.whitehouse.gov/the-press-office/president-obama-launches-educate-innovate-campaign-excellence-science-technology-en.

Ottino, J. M., & Morson, G. S. (2016, February 14). Building a bridge between engineering and the humanities. *The Chronicle of Higher Education.* Retrieved from http://chronicle.com/article/Building-a-Bridge-Between/235305.

Öztürk, M. D. (2007). Global competition: America's underrepresented minorities will be left behind. Retrieved from http://www.tcrecord.org.

Padilla, R. V., Trevino, J. [Jesus], Gonzalez, K., & Trevino, J. [Jane]. (1997). Developing local models of minority student success in college. *Journal of College Student Development, 38*(2), 125–135.

Palmer, R. T., Davis, R. J., & Hilton, A. A. (2009). Exploring challenges that threaten to impede the academic success of academically under-prepared African American male collegians at an HBCU. *Journal of College Student Development, 50,* 429–445.

Palmer, R. T., Davis, R. J., & Maramba, D. C. (2011). The impact of family support on the success of black men at a historically black university: Affirming the revision of Tinto's theory. *Journal of College Student Development, 52*(5), 577–597.

Palmer, R. T., Davis, R. J., Moore, J., III, & Hilton, A. A. (2010). A nation at risk: Increasing college participation and persistence among African American males to stimulate U.S. global competitiveness. *Journal of African American Males in Education, 1,* 105–124.

Palmer, R. T., Davis, R. J., & Thompson, T. (2010). Theory meets practice: HBCU initiatives that promote academic success among African Americans in STEM. *Journal of College Student Development, 51*(4), 440–443.

Palmer, R. T., & Gasman, M. (2008). It takes a village to raise a child: The role of social capital in promoting academic success for African American men at a Black college. *Journal of College Student Development, 49*(1), 52–70.

Palmer, R. T., Maramba, D. C., & Dancy, T. E. (2011). A qualitative investigation of factors promoting the retention and persistence of students of color in STEM. *Journal of Negro Education, 80*(4), 491–504.

Palmer, R. T., Maramba, D. C., & Holmes, L. S. (2011). A contemporary examination of factors promoting the academic success of minority students at a predominantly White university. *Journal of College Student Retention, 13*(3), 329–348.

Palmer, R. T., & Wood, J. L. (Eds.). (2012). Black men in college: Implications for HBCUs and beyond. New York, NY: Routledge.

Pascarella, E. T., & Terenzini, P. T. (2005). *How college affects students, Volume 2: A third decade of research.* San Francisco, CA: Jossey-Bass.

Perna, L. W. (2004). Understanding the decision to enroll in graduate school: Sex and racial/ethnic group differences. *Journal of Higher Education, 75*(5), 487–527.

Perna, L. W. (2006). Studying college access and choice: A proposed conceptual model. In J. C. Smart (Ed.), *Higher education: Handbook of theory and research,* Vol. XXI (pp. 99–157). Netherlands: Springer.

Perna, L., Wagner-Lundy, V., Drezner, N. D., Gasman, M., Yoon, S., Bose, E., & Gary, S. (2009). The contribution of HBCUs to the preparation of African American women for STEM careers: A case study. *Research in Higher Education, 50*(1), 1–23.

Philadelphia AMP Drexel University. (2007). Greater Philadelphia region: LSAMP. Retrieved from http://www.philadelphiaamp.org.

President's Council of Advisors on Science and Technology. (2012). Engage to excel: Producing one million additional college graduates with degrees in science, technology, engineering, and mathematics. Washington, D.C.: Author.

Purdue University. (2014). Minority engineering program. Retrieved from http://www.purdue.edu/mep.

Ramos, F., Commodore, F., & Coello, F. (n.d.). *Graduate school for students at minority serving institutions.* Retrieved from http://www2.gse.upenn.edu /cmsi/sites/gse.upenn.edu.cmsi/files/MSI_Guide2GradSchool_FINAL.pdf.

Rendón, L. I., & Hope, R. O. (Eds.). (1996). *Educating a new majority.* San Francisco, CA: Jossey-Bass.

Repko, A. F. (2012). *Interdisciplinarity: Process and theory* (2nd ed.). New York, NY: Sage.

Repko, A. F., Newell, W. H., & Szostak, R. (2011). *Case studies in interdisciplinary research.* Thousand Oaks, CA: Sage.

Ricard, R. B., & Brown, M. C. (2008). *Ebony towers in higher education: The evolution, mission, and presidency of historically Black colleges and universities.* Sterling, VA: Stylus Publishing.

Roberts, R., Phinney, J., Masse, L., Chen, Y., Roberts, C., & Romero, A. (1999). The structure of ethnic identity in young adolescents from diverse ethnocultural groups. *Journal of Early Adolescence, 19,* 301–322.

Rodriguez, J. P., Loomis, S. R., & Weeres, J. G. (2007). *The cost of institutions: Information and freedom in expanding economies.* New York, NY: Palgrave Macmillan.

Rothwell, J. (2103). The hidden STEM economy. Metropolitan Policy Program Report. Washington, D.C.: Brookings Institution.

Rovai, A. P. (2009). *The Internet and higher education: Achieving global reach.* Oxford: Elsevier.

Rovai, A. P., Ponton, M. K., & Baker, J. D. (2008). *Distance learning in higher education: A programmatic approach to planning, design, instruction, evaluation, and accreditation.* New York, NY: Teacher College Press.

Russell, M. L., & Atwater, M. M. (2005). Traveling the road to success: A disclosure on persistence throughout the science pipeline with African American students at a predominantly White institution. *Journal of Research in Science Teaching, 42*(6), 691–715.

Russell, S. H., Hancock, M. P., & McCullough, J. (2007). Benefits of undergraduate research experiences. *Science Magazine, 316*, 548–549. Retrieved from http://fhs.mcmaster.ca/pediatrics_research/documents/benefitsofundegradu ateresearchexperiencesScienceMay2007.pdf.

Science Buddies. (2015a). Explore careers in engineering. Retrieved from http://www.sciencebuddies.org/science-engineering-careers#engineering.

Science Buddies. (2015b). Explore careers in math and computer science. Retrieved from http://www.sciencebuddies.org/science-engineering-careers#math computerscience.

Science Buddies. (2015c). Explore careers in life science. Retrieved from http://www.sciencebuddies.org/science-engineering-careers#lifesciences.

Sedlacek, W. E. (1999). Black students on White campuses: 20 years of research. *Journal of college student development, 40*, 538–550.

Sedlacek, W. E. (2004a). Why we should use noncognitive variables with graduate and professional students. *The Journal of the National Association of Advisors for the Health Professions, 24*(2), 32–39.

Sedlacek, W. E. (2004b). *Beyond the big test: Noncognitive assessment in higher education*. Higher & Adult Education Series. San Francisco, CA: Jossey-Bass.

Sedlacek, W. E., Longerbeam, S. L. & Alatorre, H. A. (2003). *In their own voices: What do the data on Latino students mean to them?* (Research Report #5-02). College Park: University of Maryland Counseling Center.

Seymour, E., & Hewitt, N. M. (1997). *Talking about Leaving: Why undergraduates leave the sciences*. Oxford, U.K.: Westview Press.

Shorette, C. R., II, & Palmer, R. T. (2015). Historically Black colleges and universities (HBCUs): Critical facilitators of non-cognitive skills for Black males. *Western Journal of Black Studies, 39*(1), 18–29.

Sinek, S. (2014). *Leaders eat last deluxe: Why some teams pull together and others don't*. New York: Penguin.

Slovacek, S., Whittinghill, J., Flenoury, L., & Wiseman, D. (2012). Promoting minority success in the sciences: The minority opportunities in research programs at CSULA. *Journal of Research in Science Teaching, 49*(2), 199–217.

Smith, K. A., Sheppard, S. D., Johnson, D. W., & Johnson, R. T. (2005). Pedagogies of engagement: Classroom-based practices. *Journal of Engineering Education, 94*(1): 1–15.

Society of Women in Engineering Scholarships. (n.d.). SWE scholarships. Retrieved from http://societyofwomenengineers.swe.org/swe-scholarships.

Steele, C. (1999). A threat in the air: How stereotypes shape intellectual identity and performance. *American Psychologist, 52*(6), 613–629.

The STEM Institute. (n.d.). Retrieved from http://schools.nyc.gov/Academics /Science/SpringSTEMInstitute.htm.

Strayhorn, T. L. (2008). The role of supportive relationships in supporting African American males' success in college. *NASPA Journal, 45*, 26–48.

Strayhorn, T. L. (2010a). Work in progress: Does learning about research affect the graduate degree aspirations of STEM undergraduates? A path analysis. *Proceedings of the Frontiers in Education Conference, FIE*. Washington, D.C.: IEEE.

Strayhorn, T. L. (2010b). When race and gender collide: Social and cultural capital's influence on the academic achievement of African American and Latino males. *The Review of Higher Education, 33*(3), 307–332.

Strayhorn, T. L. (2011). Bridging the pipeline: Increasing underrepresented students' preparation for college through a summer bridge program. *American Behavioral Scientist, 55*(2), 142–159.

Strayhorn, T. (2013). *Theoretical frameworks in college student research*. Lanham, MD: University Press of America.

Strayhorn, T. L. (2015). Reframing academic advising for student success: From advisor to cultural navigator. *The Journal of the National Academic Advising Association, 35*(1), 56–63.

Supiano, B. (2015, November 10). Racial disparities in higher education: An overview. *The Chronicle of Higher Education*. Retrieved from http://chronicle .com/article/Racial-Disparities-in-Higher/234129.

Swail, W. S., Redd, K. E., & Perna, L. W. (2003). *Retaining minority students in higher education: A framework for success*. ASHE-ERIC Higher Education Report No. 2. Washington, D.C.: The George Washington University, School of Education and Human Development.

Tai, R. H., Liu, C. Q., Maltese, A. V., & Fan, X. (2006). Planning early for careers in science. *Science, 312*, 1143–1144.

Tate, F. W. (1994). Race, retrenchment, and the reform of school mathematics. *Phi Delta Kappan, 75*(6), 477–484.

Tate, F. W. (1995a). School mathematics and African American students: Thinking seriously about opportunity to learn standards. *Educational Administration Quarterly, 31*(3), 424–448.

Tate, F. W. (1995b). Returning to the root: A cultural relevant approach to mathematics pedagogy. *Theory into Practice, 34*(3), 166–173.

Tech Apprentice Program. (n.d.). Retrieved from http://www.bostonpublicschools .org/domain/1920.

Thompson, K. V., Lightfoot, N. L., Castillo, L. G., & Hurst, M. L. (2010). Influence of family perceptions of acting White on acculturative stress in African American college students. *International Journal for the Advancement of Counseling, 32*(2), 144–152.

Tinto, V. (1993). *Leaving college: Rethinking the causes and cures of student attrition* (Vol. 2). Chicago, IL: University of Chicago Press.

Tinto, V. (2012). *Completing college: Rethinking institutional action.* Chicago, IL: The University of Chicago Press.

Tornatzky, L. E., Macias, D. J., & Solis, C. (2006). *Access and achievement: Building educational and career pathways for Latinos in advanced technology.* Los Angeles, CA: Tomas Rivera Policy Institute.

Tulgan, B. (2007). Accountability should be the standard for managers as well as employees. *Employment Relations Today, 34*(2), 21–28.

Tyson, K., Darity W., & Castellino, D. R. (2005). It's not "a Black Thing": Understanding the burden of acting White and other dilemmas of high achievement. *American Sociological Review, 70*, 582–605.

Tyson, W., Lee, R., Borman, K. M., & Hanson, M. A. (2007). Science, technology, engineering, and mathematics (STEM) pathways: High school science and math coursework and postsecondary degree attainment. *Journal of Education for Students Placed at Risk, 12*(3), 243–270.

UCI Ayala School of Biological Sciences. (2014). UCI outreach, research training and minority science programs: About. Retrieved from http://port.bio.uci.edu/about/.

UNCF-Merck Undergrad Science Research Scholarship Awards. (n.d.). Scholarships and fellowships. Retrieved from http://umsi.uncf.org/sif.

United Negro College Fund-STEM Scholarship. (n.d.). Retrieved from https://scholarships.uncf.org/.

University of California, Santa Cruz. (2015). Academic excellence program. Retrieved from http://ace.ucsc.edu.

University Herald. (2012, December 4). XULA beats Ivy League schools in highest Black STEM graduates. Retrieved from http://www.universityherald.com/articles/2625/20121204/xavier-university-louisiana-highest-number-stem-graduates.htm.

University of Dayton. (2016). School of engineering. Minority engineering program. Retrieved from https://www.udayton.edu/engineering/diversity/minority-engineering/index.php.

University of Washington. (2016). PNW LSAMP: UW Louis Stokes alliance for minority participation. Retrieved from http://depts.washington.edu/lsamp.

U.S. Bureau of Labor Statistics. (2012). Employment projections program (employment, projections, and education data) and occupational employment statistics survey (wage data). Retrieved from http://www.bls.gov/opub/mlr/2012/01/art5full.pdf.

U.S. Bureau of Labor Statistics. (2014). Annual Average. Table 5. Employment Status of the Population by Sex, Marital Status, and Presence and Age of Own Children Under 18, 2012–2013. Retrieved from http://www.bls.gov/news.release/famee.t05.htm.

U.S. Census Bureau. (2008). U.S. Hispanic population surpasses 45 million: Now 15 percent of total. *U.S. Census Bureau News.* Washington, D.C.: U.S. Department of Commerce. Retrieved from http://www.prnewswire.com/news-releases/us-hispanic-population-surpasses-45-million-57046462.html.

U.S. Census Bureau. (2012). Most children younger than age 1 are minorities, Census Bureau reports. Retrieved from https://www.census.gov/newsroom/releases/archives/population/cb12-90.html.

U.S. Department of Education. (2000). *Entry and persistence of women and minorities in college science and engineering education.* Washington, D.C.: Author.

U.S. Department of Education. (n.d.). White house initiative on historically Black colleges and universities: HBCUs and 2020 goal. Retrieved from http://sites.ed.gov/whhbcu.

Vanderbilt University School of Medicine. (2016). Vanderbilt summer science academy: Minority engineering programs. Retrieved from https://www.engr.ncsu.edu/mep.

Varma, R. (2009). Attracting Native Americans to computing. *Communication of the ACM, 52*(8), 137–140.

VIP Women in Technology Scholarship Program. (n.d.). Retrieved from http://www.trustvip.com/news/press-releases/vip-announces-2016-women-in-technology-scholarship-wits-program/.

Washington, J. (2011). Declining numbers of Blacks seen in math, science. Huffington Post. Retrieved from http://www.huffingtonpost.com/huff-wires/20111023/us-blacks-in-math-and-science-/.

Watson, L. W. (2006). The role of spirituality and religion in the experiences of African American male college students. In M. J. Cuyjet (Ed.), *African American men in college* (pp. 112–127). San Francisco, CA: Jossey-Bass.

Wei, C. C., & Carroll, C. D. (2004). *A decade of undergraduate student aid: 1989–90 to 1999–2000.* Washington, D.C.: National Center for Education Statistics.

White House. (n.d.). Educate to innovate. Retrieved from https://www.whitehouse.gov/issues/education/k-12/educate-innovate.

White House. (2016). STEM for all. Retrieved from https://www.whitehouse.gov/blog/2016/02/11/stem-all.

Whiting, G. W. (2006). Promoting a scholar identity among African American males: Implications for gifted education. *Gifted Education Press Quarterly, 20*(3), 2–6.

Williams, A., & Justice, M. (2010). Attitudes of African American males regarding counseling in four Texas universities. *Education, 131*(1), 158–168.

Williams, D. G., & Land, R. R. (2006). The legitimation of Black subordination: The impact of color-blind ideology on African American education. *Journal of Negro Education, 75*(4), 579.

Wines, M. (2015, November 10). A real Missouri "concerned student 1950" speaks, at age 89. *The New York Times.* Retrieved from http://www.nytimes.com/2015/11/11/us/an-original-missouri-concerned-student-1950-speaks-at-age-89.html?smprod=nytcore-iphone&smid=nytcore-iphone-share&_r=0ay.

Wood, J. L., & Harris, F., III. (2013). The community college survey of men: An initial validation of the instrument's non-cognitive outcomes construct. *Community College Journal of Research and Practice, 37*, 333–338.

Wood, J. L., & Palmer, R. T. (2015). *Black men in higher education: A guide to ensuring student success*. New York, NY: Routledge.

Xerox Technical Minority Scholarship. (n.d.). Retrieved from http://www.xerox .com/jobs/minority-scholarships/enus.html.

Yosso, T. Y. (2005). Whose culture has capital? A critical race theory discussion of community cultural wealth. *Race Ethnicity and Education, 8*(1), 69–91.

About the Authors

Robert T. Palmer is an associate professor in the Department of Educational Leadership and Policy Studies at Howard University. His research examines issues of access, equity, retention, persistence, and the college experience of racial and ethnic minorities, particularly within the context of historically Black colleges and universities. Dr. Palmer's work has been published in leading journals in higher education, such as the *Journal of College Student Development, Teachers College Record, Journal of Diversity in Higher Education, Journal of Negro Education, College Student Affairs Journal, Journal of College Student Retention,* the *Negro Educational Review,* and *Journal of Black Studies,* among others. Since earning his PhD in 2007, Dr. Palmer has authored/co-authored more than 100 academic publications. His books include *Racial and Ethnic Minority Students' Success in STEM Education* (2011, Jossey-Bass), *Black Men in College: Implications for HBCUs and Beyond* (2012, Routledge), *Black Graduate Education at HBCUs: Trends, Experiences, and Outcomes* (2012, Information Age Publishing), *Fostering Success of Ethnic and Racial Minorities in STEM: The Role of Minority Serving Institutions* (2012, Routledge), *Community Colleges and STEM: Examining Underrepresented Racial and Ethnic Minorities* (2013, Routledge), *STEM Models of Success: Programs, Policies, and Practices* (2014, Information Age Press), *Black Male Collegians: Increasing Access, Retention, and Persistence in Higher Education* (2014, Jossey-Bass), *Understanding HIV and STI Prevention for College Students* (2014, Routledge), *Black Men in Higher Education: A Guide to Ensuring Success* (2014, Routledge), *Exploring Diversity at Historically Black Colleges and Universities: Implications for Policy and Practice* (2015, Jossey-Bass), *Hispanic Serving Institutions: Their Origin, and Present and Future Challenges* (2015, Stylus), *Black Men in the Academy: Stories of Resiliency, Inspiration, and Success* (2015, Palgrave Macmillan), and *Graduate Education at HBCUs: The*

Student Perspective (Routledge, forthcoming). In 2009, the American College Personnel Association's (ACPA) Standing Committee for Men recognized his excellent research on Black men with its Outstanding Research Award. In 2011, Dr. Palmer was named an ACPA Emerging Scholar, and, in 2012, he received the Carlos J. Vallejo Award of Emerging Scholarship from the American Education Research Association (AERA). In 2012, he was also awarded the Association for the Study of Higher Education (ASHE)-Mildred García Junior Exemplary Scholarship Award. In 2015, Diverse Issues in Higher Education recognized Dr. Palmer as an emerging scholar. Later that year, he also received the SUNY Chancellor's award for Excellence in Scholarship and Creative Activities. This prestigious award is normally given to a full professor.

Andrew T. Arroyo is an associate professor of Interdisciplinary Studies and co-director for Learning Communities at Norfolk State University, a public historically Black university. Prior to becoming a professor, he spent 13 years in the private sector running for-profit businesses and nonprofit community organizations. His research addresses themes of diversity and inclusion, and it can be found in such journals as the *American Journal of Education, Journal of Diversity in Higher Education, Journal of College Student Retention, Journal of Transformative Education, Spectrum: A Journal on Black Men, Learning Communities Journal,* and *Teaching Theology and Religion,* among others. He is currently co-authoring *Black Female College Students: A Guide to Student Success in Higher Education* (Routledge), and co-editing *Effective Leadership at Minority Serving Institutions: Exploring Opportunities and Challenges for Leadership* (Routledge). Dr. Arroyo is program director for NSU's Classroom to Careers Pipeline, which is funded in part by the UNCF's Career Pathways Initiative Grant, and designed to place NSU's graduates into meaningful careers in their chosen fields.

Alonzo M. Flowers III is an assistant professor in the School of Education at Drexel University. Dr. Flowers specializes in educational issues, including academic identity development of African American and Latino males in STEM education. He also focuses on issues such as diversity, teaching and learning, and college student development. Specifically, Dr. Flowers' research focuses on the academic experiences of academically gifted African American male students in the STEM disciplines. Dr. Flowers was selected to join the Massachusetts Institute for College and Career Readiness (MICCR) at Boston University in the Senior Research Fellows program. To date, he has completed 40 peer-reviewed national conference presentations, including several presentations at the Association for the Study of Higher Education (ASHE) and American Educational Research Association (AERA). In 2014, Dr. Flowers served as one of the keynote speakers at the first annual Texas African American Males in College Achievement & Success Symposium in Austin, Texas, where he discussed "Giftedness at a Crossroads for African American Male College Students in STEM." Dr. Flowers is also a member of the *Journal of Race and Policy* editorial board. Additionally, he is a reviewer for several educational journals, including the *Journal of African American Males in Education* (JAAME). Dr. Flowers' research continues to impact the needs of underrepresented students in education as he has authored or co-authored several book chapters and articles that focus on students of color and their academic experiences. Dr. Flowers has presented at several local, state, national, and international conferences. Some of his presentations included Gifted, African American, and Males in Engineering; Understanding the Gifted Poor; From Big Man on Campus to Metrosexuals: Exploring the Changes in the Perception of Masculinity for College Males; The Completion Barrier: Why Hispanic Students Fall off the College Map; and Not Finishing the Academic Race: What Is Keeping Minority Students from Reaching the Finish Line?

Index

Page numbers followed by *t* indicate tables and *f* indicate figures.

FEB 1 0 2018